D1553151

Renner Learning Resource Center
Elgin Community College
Elgin, IL 60123

Ten Unknowns

By the same author

Plays

Mizlansky/Zilinsky or; "Schmucks"

The Film Society

The Substance of Fire

The End of the Day

Three Hotels

A Fair Country

Hedda Gabler

The Paris Letter

Chinese Friends

Screenplays

The Substance of Fire

People I Know

JON ROBIN BAITZ

Ten Unknowns

Grove Press
New York

FIRST EDITION

Library of Congress Cataloging-in-Publication Data

Baitz, Jon Robin, 1961-
    Ten unknowns / by Jon Robin Baitz.— 1st ed.
        p. cm.
    ISBN 0-8021-3827-6
    1. Americans—Mexico—Drama. 2. Women art students—
Drama. 3. Painters—Drama. 4. Mexico—Drama. 5. Exiles—
Drama. I. Title: 10 unknowns. II. Title.

    PS3552.A393T46 2004
    812'.54—dc22

                                                              2003056910

Grove Press
841 Broadway
New York, NY 10003

04 05 06 07 08   10 9 8 7 6 5 4 3 2 1

Ten Unknowns was first presented at Lincoln Center Theater (Andre Bishop, artistic director) in New York City on March 8, 2001. It was directed by Daniel Sullivan; the set design was by Ralph Funicello; the lighting design was by Pat Collins; the music was by Robert Waldman; the costume design was by Jess Goldstein; and the stage manager was Roy Harris. The cast was as follows:

TREVOR FABRICANT	Denis O'Hare
MALCOLM RAPHELSON	Donald Sutherland
JUDD STURGESS	Justin Kirk
JULIA BRYANT	Juliana Margulies

Ten Unknowns was then presented at the Huntington Theatre Company (Nicholas Martin, artistic director) in Boston on May 22, 2002. It was directed by Evan Yinoulis; the set design was by Adam Stockhausen; the lighting design was by Donald Holder; the music was by Rick Baitz; the costume design was by Tom Broeker; and the stage manager was Thomas M. Kauffman. The cast was as follows:

TREVOR FABRICANT	T. Scott Cunningham
MALCOLM RAPHELSON	Ron Rifkin
JUDD STURGESS	Jonathan M. Woodward
JULIA BRYANT	Kathryn Hahn

Ten Unknowns was presented in a West Coast premiere at the Mark Taper Forum (Gordon Davidson, artistic director/producer) in Los Angeles on March 27, 2003. It was directed by Robert Egan; the set design was by David Jenkins; the lighting design was by Michael Gilliam; the sound design was by Jon Gottlieb; the costume design was by Joyce Kim Lee; and the stage manager was Mary K. Klinger. The cast was as follows:

TREVOR FABRICANT	Patrick Breen
MALCOLM RAPHELSON	Stacy Keach
JUDD STURGESS	Jonathan M. Woodward
JULIA BRYANT	Klea Scott

A Note on the Play

The smart thing for a playwright to do is let a play speak for itself without comment from its author, but *Ten Unknowns* has the problem of requiring actual paintings in it; hence this note.

One day in the early 1980s, I was visiting the Los Angeles County Museum of Art with an acquaintance, an elderly painter who worked in quiet and absolute obscurity on a side street in West Los Angeles, in a studio surrounded by quaint Japanese nurseries. We stopped in front of a small drawing, a Corot, I think. My companion stood in front of it for a very long time, staring sadly, then blankly into space. Eventually he smiled and explained: "I used to own this." Twenty or so years ago, when he had a little money from selling his own work, he had bought art, and when his own work stopped selling, he had to divest himself of his beloved collection simply in order to live. The sorrow of his story was piercing to me, and I made a note of it at the time in my on-and-off-again journal. As a young writer all of twenty-three, I felt witness to a sobering object lesson in the—possibly very short—life span of an artist's creative powers, the myth of ownership, and what life is like after you've cracked. The message was portentous to me: "This will be you—it is not a matter of if; merely when. He is you." And indeed, I often go totally mute for long periods. Raphelson's and Judd's struggles are mine.

My elderly artist friend in L.A. came out of the school known as "Bay Area Figuration," which refers to a group of artists working in and around San Francisco who made a sometimes tortured shift out of abstraction into figuration at the beginning of the 1950s. These painters include David Park (1911–60), who was the oldest of the group, Elmer Bischoff (1916–91), and Richard Diebenkorn (1922–93), who moved away from figuration into a singularly thrilling language of abstraction that seemed to capture the light and topography of California in an entirely new way. Many of these painters taught or studied at the California School of Fine Arts (CSFA). Clyfford Still (1904-80), who was on the faculty, was a star abstract expressionist and hugely influential in his bellicose disdain for figurative work. Diebenkorn's figurative period lasted only a decade before he moved back to abstraction, where he had started his career. Take a look at his representational painting, alongside that of Park's from the same period, and then look at a Diebenkorn after he returned to abstraction, and it may help illuminate exactly what happened to Malcolm Raphelson—or at least, what he may have felt.

The anguished search for a personal style is a recurring theme in the Bay Area art of that period. David Park had worked diligently for four years as an abstract painter, and then one day in 1949, he drove to the San Francisco dump and threw out all his nonrepresentational painting. Four years later in an art magazine he explained: "I was concerned with big abstract ideals like vitality, energy, profundity, warmth. They became my gods. They still are. I disciplined myself to work in ways I hoped might symbolize those ideals. I still hold to those ideals today, but I realize that those paintings practically never, even vaguely, approximated any achievement of my aims. Quite the opposite: What the paintings told me was that I was a hardworking guy who was trying to be important."

Trying to be important is a terrible trap and zero-sum game for an artist of any age. The despondency, not to mention possible liberation, of Park's act figured in the conceptualization of this play, which, ultimately, is a self-portrait of the artist as young/old man. To be a blocked artist is to have a disease: Almost blind, often numb, you don't stop wanting to make art. The hunger remains—not merely for redemption or recognition, but also, at least in the case of Raphelson, for revenge.

Which brings me back to the paintings in the play. I think of pictures in the style of Park and Bischoff married to those of Eric

Fischl (1948–), a contemporary artist whose work of the early eighties has much of the raw and exuberant roughness I imagine for the shotgun-marriage paintings of Judd and Raphelson.

Jon Robin Baitz
New York City
June 1, 2002

This play is for my father,
Edward Baitz (1922–2001)

TEN UNKNOWNS

1992. An artist's studio in a decrepit house in a village in central Mexico. A chaotic room. Upstage there is a rack, with eight paintings, none of which are visible. There are some comforts, a sofa, piles of records and books, but it's not luxurious, it's squalid. MALCOLM RAPHELSON, *in his seventies, with a shock of white hair, is drinking mescal and talking to* TREVOR FABRICANT, *an Anglified South African who wears a somewhat impractical European suit, and who has about him an almost Mahler-like intensity.*

FABRICANT   But Malcolm, all we're talking about is a quick trip. We'll put you up in a nice hotel—

RAPHELSON   Hey, I'm sorry but it's a lot to throw at me, son.

FABRICANT   Nevertheless, you'd find New York exciting now.

RAPHELSON   Oh I don't think so, Trevor.

FABRICANT   No, there's a kind of quiet revolt going on.

RAPHELSON   Yeah? How quiet? Are we changing the length of skirts again? Is it that kind of quiet, or is it "no more tail-fins."

FABRICANT   *(Ignoring Raphe.)*   There is this sense: the sense that this madness has gone too far. That the experiments are riddled with failure. The Whitney Biennial, I think, is what pushed it over the edge.

RAPHELSON   Well it would be that, wouldn't it? The Biennial. That would do it. Look. I ain't goin' home.

FABRICANT   How interesting that in fact you still call it home. I haven't been back to Cape Town in sixteen years and I do the same thing. It's so very difficult, to be so foreign all the time.

RAPHELSON   I'm sure in your case, that is true.

FABRICANT   What I'm getting at is that we are at a crossroads.

RAPHELSON   Yes? We meaning you and I or we meaning "the world as a whole"?

FABRICANT   Please stop being dodgy and evasive, Malcolm.

RAPHELSON   I don't know how you got this idea that I could be induced back to the States. You know I am allergic to the American enthusiasms: I break out, I break out in embarrassment all over.

FABRICANT   Yes, but when you were painting, when you were in your WPA period, you did not.

RAPHELSON   I was younger. I still had certain beliefs.

FABRICANT   Isn't it interesting to examine through your work, how you got to this odd place? Because you were singled out for praise.

RAPHELSON   Yeah I was, right, over a year ago, at an insignificant little back room of a show at a minor dusty old—

FABRICANT   (*Over him.*)   The Smithsonian Public Arts Retrospective—is hardly—It's how I heard of you in the first place, some cobweb-filled academic actually *did* some work, dug out one of your pictures, and *voilà,* and I unearthed you . . .

RAPHELSON   Trevor! We are talking about minor work from the nineteen forties!

FABRICANT   Precisely. Then help me change that! That you are not merely a "what became of" . . . ? You've been down here, in this exile, working away, and now that you've been located, why wouldn't you want to share what you've been doing *all this time*?

RAPHELSON   "All this time"? I take a lot of siestas, son.

FABRICANT   Yes, I'll admit there have been fallow periods. But there is a body of work. This is why this is the moment—the exact moment to plan to put together a little show of some of the old and some of the *new* work—

RAPHELSON   (*Scornful. Dismissing his oeuvre.*)   "Work." Jesus. Scratchings, daubings, and sex-trash.

FABRICANT   Nevertheless. Since I've sent Judd to assist you've somehow rather heroically generated eight pictures, which I am on the cusp of moving. (*He points towards the rack of paintings.*)   New work. On the basis of your having been singled out in Washington, D.C.

Beat. Raphelson shrugs. He pours a drink. He drinks. He drinks more. He shrugs.

FABRICANT   (*cont.*)   But of course timing is everything. Timing, Malcolm. This, I know. At my grandfather's vineyard outside Cape Town, I grew up watching him study the conditions, trying to calculate the best time to pick the grapes. The exact hour when the sugar is at the right level. It makes all the difference. The exact moment meant prosperity for another year.

RAPHELSON   Yeah, grapes. Hard to grow; 'course down in South Africa there you had lotsa kaffirs to help out, all that crushing, right? And of course, they were thrilled to make a nice Côte du Rhône for all you white settlers.

3

Beat.

FABRICANT   Point taken. You are not a grape. And I have apologized for being South African many times. I will not apologize for encouraging you to leave this absurd place, this absurd dusty obscurity. This penance.

RAPHELSON   Look, I think we're working at cross-purposes. I don't think these pictures are what I want them to be.

FABRICANT   You know what I found, I found this in a junk shop in Hudson, New York. (*He picks up a small cardboard tube, and unravels a small poster.*)   "Ten Unknowns of 1949." My God.

Raphelson displays no interest in the poster after taking it in.

RAPHELSON   Yeah.

FABRICANT   And now here we are in 1992. Forty-three years later. You were part of the last great social art movement in our history. Forty-three years later. Narcissism and self love, and isn't it time to look at what's come in between? An American artist with this exile's perspective. Look at the names on this poster. Only one is recognizable. A mediocre figurative painter who hid her lack of talent in abstract expressionism.

RAPHELSON   Yeah, well, that's what it was sorta there for. Abstract expressionism. "We've run outta ideas—let's try a giant slash of *green*—for man and God and little girls, "We're new and furious and we just started to notice that modern light hits us *differently* than it used to," giant blur of cadmium red. It was a cargo cult then, and it is now. False gods and idol worship.

FABRICANT   No. That's my point, isn't it?

4

RAPHELSON (*A deep scorn.*) "Abstract expressionism." Yes, some of them, some of them were onto something great. Sorrow. Mystery, yes. Sure. But more often than not, you could make a little jump into shit-shaped daubing, into splotches and batches of half-baked color, and you'd win a Cracker Jack prize. And you had to do it or you were out.

FABRICANT But the boy. Let's—let's talk about Judd for a moment. This boy I sent, I had doubts but he seemed to have worked out, tell me so I may put my doubts aside finally, Mal. He's helped, eh?

RAPHELSON Well it ain't easy havin' some sarcastic little shit here sneering, I can tell you that. But. I like him.

FABRICANT He's been useful, right? I have this funny Jewish matchmaker thing, I thought you'd do well together.

RAPHELSON He could even make a half-decent painter one day.

FABRICANT There is the question of focus.

RAPHELSON If he ever figures out who he is.

FABRICANT Show me what you've been doing. Stop hiding this work from me, I don't wish to be subtle with you and manipulate you, so I'll tell you, I need to see the big landscape.

RAPHELSON (*Cool.*) Not quite ready yet, pal.

FABRICANT I brought you cash for that new drawing you allowed me to sell. You will notice that there are some thousands of dollars in this envelope. And I says this without editorial prejudice.

He takes an envelope out of his jacket. Malcolm doesn't take it. Fabricant puts it on the table.

FABRICANT (*cont.*)   The money will continue to multiply. If you allow me to build the brand, the Raphelson brand.

RAPHELSON   You think I want that? I'm not saying I don't need it, but you won't hook me with money.

FABRICANT   Money? Heaven forbid. We hate money, we reject it, we talk today of truth. But. Look, sometimes buying thing makes up for some of the other holes. A cashmere sweater, say, or sex. (*In my case.*)   Buy something. There must be things you want.

RAPHELSON (*Smiling. Staring at Fabricant.*)   Ohhh. Just one thing, at the moment. (*A sigh. Looks at the money.*)   For so long I was actually starving. I had to count every cent. I begged once. I did drawings and sold them to touristas for six months. Yeah. And then I sold everything in this room, basically for scraps, over the years. (*Beat.*)   The old gringo painter; stop five on the bus on the way to visit the big tree.

FABRICANT   The fact is that the bus no longer stops here, Mal. I understand the reflex towards parsimony. I understand it, but it's a phantom limb, it's not needed anymore.

RAPHELSON   Of course, you know, things are changing down here. Everything suddenly costs more because the Americans have discovered the place and so we have tour busses and magazine people and travelling pederasts and Texans and shit. (*Beat.*)   Sometimes I think the only thing to do is keep movin' south like some German war criminal. (*He pockets the money.*)   Away from whatever this particular national cancer brings . . . y'know?

JUDD STURGESS *enters. In his late twenties or thereabouts, carrying a Mexican shopping bag. He is wearing the ruins of a once fantastic black suit and tee shirt, work boots, all of which are paint splattered. Dogs bark from off as he comes in.*

JUDD (*Yelling off.*) Shut up. (*To Trevor and Raphe.*) One of those fucks tried to bite me. A little one.

RAPHELSON That's how it works, kid.

JUDD The girl isn't here yet?

RAPHELSON Any minute.

FABRICANT More guests?

JUDD Yeah, Mal found some girl from San Francisco. You think he sent me out to get wine and cheese and stuff for *you?*

He puts the package down on the table.

RAPHELSON She's very lovely, both of you, you'll see. Yeah, I found this kid in the square, in the *zocalo,* she's something, she's a biologist from Berkeley, and she needed help . . . she clearly required assistance.

JUDD I'm sure.

RAPHELSON Yeah, and she had this thing that just got right under my skin. When I stumbled into her. A John O'Hara girl fumbling in her phrase book, for the word for "photosynthesis." (*Beat.*) I'm going to paint her.

JUDD (*Busying himself with cleaning brushes.*) Oh. Hey. Wow. A subject?

RAPHELSON Well, I intend to find out. There used to be people like her, you know—women—in particular, who had been through the war, and what came after, all the red crap. Strong people, took no shit.

JUDD Huh.

RAPHELSON (*Taking in Judd and Fab.*) The breed has been lost, I think.

JUDD Oh, yeah, we're all sorta sucky now. (*Wheeling on Trevor.*) Trevor, muthafucka, you were supposed to bring me a VCR, some magazines, and some Pop-Tarts. And you brought nothing.

FABRICANT (*Reaching to his pocket.*) Here. Aero-Mexico peanuts. (*He tosses them to Judd.*) Judd. Malcolm won't let me see the new work.

JUDD Right. Well. Gotta be patient. He has a different clock than you're used to.

RAPHELSON Judd, so . . . you agree with your boss, is this the moment for a triumphant return . . . ?

JUDD (*Careful and casual.*) Hey man. It's not like they're giving you, like the big room at MOMA. Whenever you're ready, stick a toe in. If you're wigged out by the idea, pass. You know, you've gone this long without. So. No biggie, is it?

There is silence. Fabricant would like to kill Judd.

JUDD (*cont.*) (*Taking in his employer's dissatisfaction with this answer.*) Be sad though to let it all slip away.

FABRICANT Thank you Judd, for that ringing endorsement. Why must—why do you mock everything?

JUDD Mal, defend me to Trev.

RAPHELSON   Oh, yeah, he's great. He has strong arms. He's good at lifting and mixing paints and chattering.

JUDD   See? I'm good at "chattering." You think you could write that in a letter of recommendation when I leave here?

RAPHELSON   Are you nuts? When you leave? You think I'm going to give you anything, kid?

JUDD   Not even one of these cute paintings?

Raphelson smiles. This is a game between these two.

RAPHELSON   Judd: Let me tell you a little story. Rauschenberg asked de Kooning for a a drawing, this is early on, a little gift, a gesture. So, you know, de Kooning is flattered, and obliges him, and Rauschenberg takes this drawing and spends ages erasing it. Obliterating it entirely. This I think was an act of war.

JUDD   Maybe Rauschenberg was asking for help. And maybe that was the only way available to him to try and understand an artist he admired? Because de Kooning was parsimonious, private and—

Pause.

RAPHELSON   Which was his right. Look. Bending over to be charitable, the kindest interpretation is that it was a challenge from one generation to the other. And who wants to be challenged?

JUDD   Yeah, no way it could have possibly been love, right? Wanting to know someone you're amazed by, could it?

RAPHELSON   Christ. You think there's fellow feeling in the art world? You think artists, artists want to share . . . ? This is the view that only a homosexual could have.

9

JUDD   Right. But maybe Rauschenberg was enacting an homage. Maybe he was looking for ways to get in beneath the surface texture—

RAPHELSON   Or maybe he was killing daddy.

FABRICANT   (*Who wants to get back to his point.*)   But the fact is, this is all ancient history. Think of what you've been through and where we are headed. Has not the worst already happened to you?

RAPHELSON   (*A smile. Looks at Judd.*)   Oh who knows, you can never tell.

FABRICANT   And what you've survived tells a story. In exile, disgusted with the American maw, a man of integrity flees, and is found in the wilderness, filled with vigor and vitality, and reawakened . . .

RAPHELSON   Like Rip van Winkle. It's like something from *Look* magazine circa 1958.

FABRICANT   The truth is, this lack of trust on your part is no longer called for. Not here, not with me. I know things which you should not know. I sold a picture to a movie star last year. A very good Leon Kossoff. And this star had recently had a comeback, All of a sudden he has a success in a movie where he literally spoke half a dozen or so sentences. But was the silent center of the action.

   And he explained to me—that he had finally figured it out. Get a new agent, someone young, and clever, and let the picture do the work. The point is trusting that others might know more about timing and striking than you.

RAPHELSON   Look. I'm not gonna be able to stand in some fucking gallery smiling with a cracker while those awful people—

FABRICANT (*Cutting him off. Exploding, utterly furious, frightening.*)   Judd can hold the crackers! I can! Nothing more is required of you, damn it, you've done your work, I'm not going to treat you like a circus freak, you think so little of me? I should just leave you to your squalor then—

He stops. Raphelson is grinning. He loves this.

JUDD   Look, Mal. Show him what you've been working on. The man has come all the way here from goddamn Wooster Street to see you.

RAPHELSON   When I started painting again, it had been so long . . . and so I dunno. These things, even though they're big and they have a kind of drama . . . deep down I think they're just transitional. I don't quite believe in this yet.

FABRICANT   You might have said something to that effect before I came all the way down here. I was on a bus next to a quadruped for eight hours. A quadruped who defecated on my shoe.

RAPHELSON   I warned you, Trevor, that this was uncertain. This entire experiment. In promotion.

JULIA (*From off.*)   Hello. Is this it?

RAPHELSON (*Calling out.*)   Yeah, we're in here.

JUDD (*Quietly, grinning.*)   Target acquired.

JULIA BRYANT, *30, enters. She wears old well-worn khakis, an old white tee shirt and running shoes, no adornment.*

RAPHELSON   Come in . . . ?

JULIA (*Entering, smiling, flustered.*)   The streets. No signs, nothing.

RAPHELSON   No, no signs. It's better that way.

JULIA   But those that do have signs are all called Jalisco or Juarez. Oh boy, and my cartoon Spanish keeps failing me, totally. I—I— finally stopped in at this little store, down the hill, the lady by the way said you owe her, I think twenty thousand dollars or something, not sure . . . (*Beat.*)   God. Listen to me. I've been alone for too long, I see people and I get overstimulated.

JUDD   Yeah, Ritalin's good for that. I grew up on the stuff. I'm Judd.

JULIA   Oh, yes, the assistant. I'm Julia.

RAPHELSON   And this is Trevor Fabricant, who has just arrived a few hours ago from New York. And is disrupting everything.

JUDD   And who will soon get pretty sick, which will be so much fun.

FABRICANT   No, I'm from Africa. Cast-iron stomach. Besides, if I do get ill, it's a small price to pay for culture. (*To Julia.*)   Yet another American on the run?

JULIA   No, not on the run, actually.

RAPHELSON   She's down at the lake trying to save some frogs.

JULIA   Not so much saving. Salvation is too grand. Plus. It's maybe too late. There is a growing consensus about the "e" word.

JUDD   For . . . extinction?

FABRICANT   Yes, I read about this in the *Times,* reptiles on the decline, was quite alarmed, thought it was about art dealers or something. Are you a professor, then?

JULIA No. Just a lowly teaching assistant doing grad work. They do this thing, the professors, they send you to uncomfortable places on their behalf and then if the news is interesting, they come down later and take all the credit. (*Beat.*) It's very lovely back here. Hidden away.

RAPHELSON I've been here twenty-eight years. When I first rented it, I paid eight dollars a month. Which I didn't have, but still. I took a deep breath and have never left. (*For Trevor.*) It's home.

JULIA Have you not been back to the States in twenty-eight years?

RAPHELSON Since '63.

JULIA The year I was born.

RAPHELSON Thanks. Tell me. Have I missed much? I mean, Johnson was just getting started on Vietnam. I've managed to miss Nixon, Reagan, Bush, born-again Christians, and performance artists. Am I leaving anything out that brings us up to 1992?

JULIA No, that's pretty much it, you hit the main points.

JUDD This is a long game, Julia. "Reasons never to return." But followed by wistful talk about the "village, my old walk up on East Third, Boyle Heights when I was a kid."

RAPHELSON Yes, the things I miss.

JUDD "My studio on La Brea. The Cedar Tavern. The Waldorf cafeteria."

RAPHELSON Some little things I miss. Yes. Not much more.

JULIA I was having street tacos yesterday, and they were so great, and I strangely found myself, like mid-bite, missing the Tex-Mex place on my corner in Berkeley.

FABRICANT How long are you here for?

JULIA Oh. The mating season is half over.

JUDD You have a mating season?

JULIA (*A small smile.*) Well, I very well may, but that's not the point. If they don't show up, if it's past hope . . . and I have no hard numbers, I'll have to pack up in a month. Not by choice. The department will pull my funding.
    But I'd like to stay on, chart it, write about it, and see if it can't be fixed elsewhere.

RAPHELSON And honestly, you're living in one of those shacks by the lake?

JULIA It's cheap. The study of vanishing amphibians is not lucrative. Pandas and tigers get star billing. We're poor, we make do with scraps. I've been looking to rent a room in a house in town.

Raphelson shrugs.

RAPHELSON Yes, right, there are several nice people, Señora Guzzman has a very nice room which you could share with her daughter—and their donkey. (*He pours wine, hands her the glass.*) I don't see why you shouldn't be comfortable. (*Beat.*) It's—the see-through frogs you're looking for, yes? I used to see them all the time.

JULIA But not for a while, right? They look like emeralds. We call them "jewels of the night." A few years ago there was a sudden drop in amphibious population levels.

JUDD   And we're next to go, is that it?

JULIA   Oh, I think at some point. Maybe. Not next Thursday. But . . . the frogs are kind of a bellwether for so *many* things and so you start to ask "well, *okay, what* are they telling us. Are these conditions reversible?" You know. Not that self-interest is the point, but . . . somehow this idea of warnings has not caught on. People are underwhelmed.

RAPHELSON   It's probably just a matter of deciding which horrors to notice and which to ignore.

JULIA   Yes. Too much bad news. And so hard to compete with sexier, shorter, more bite-sized stories, and also, I've noticed, in Mexico this is not a subject suitable for women.

RAPHELSON   You should also remember that the currency is different here.

FABRICANT   Maybe it just started getting too crowded.

JUDD   And the frogs moved somewhere less frantic.

JULIA   This isn't getting any press play (*God knows why*), but some hotel chain from Arizona has been stocking the lake with bass for sports-fishermen from Texas. They're planning to build a sort of theme-park with pink stucco fish or something. And those bass eat froggies like they're popcorn.

RAPHELSON   People down here need money too, you know. You can hardly begrudge the locals for wanting some of that dinero from up north.

JUDD   Yeah. I want some too.

JULIA   Of course. But if it's this wholesale slaughter of species going on without even the merest thought of having an environmental impact report done . . .

RAPHELSON   Well, what would it matter, it's Mexico, someone would have paid someone else off, the fights are fixed, no point in fighting that.

JUDD   Yes. No. None.

FABRICANT   Survival of the fittest.

RAPHELSON   I'm just sayin'; them pastel condos are goin' up and them frogs is goin' to Guatemala.

JUDD   Malcolm loves Armageddon scenarios; they have a kind of kiddie porn appeal to him.

RAPHELSON   Okay. (*Patiently.*)   The vanity of Americans buying up a place and at the same time, sending missionaries down to save it, is an old and sorry tradition, we know this, we all know that.

JULIA   Yes. I am aware of that. I am not down here for salvation. I'm down here for survival. I am naive in certain ways, maybe, but not that one, period. If anything can be done, it's by literally thousands of people with one idea: Map the conditions, analyze the data, and maybe turn things around. No single "I." And no biblical implications.

RAPHELSON   (*Almost over her.*)   But—the question being asked of you—the question you have to deal with—"is why we should trust you?" "What are you offering?"

JULIA   I am gathering knowledge. No. I'm taking nothing. I am studying a horrible situation, and . . . the conditions. Which, if people understood . . .

RAPHELSON   More taking. More colonialism.

There is a sudden flood of something of within here, which is hard to hide.

JULIA So you guys all think . . . don't bother?

JUDD *"Me."* Don't bother me, is what I think. I am kidding, I think it's probably too late to do anything about *everything*.

RAPHELSON (*Ignoring Judd.*) There are endings, aren't there, to life? You learn to be fatalistic. Things die off. There are endings.

JULIA Yes, I agree, so . . . you're saying it's easier, it's less taxing, God knows *less risky*, to be a spectator . . . ?

RAPHELSON It has nothing to do with effort; if it's the end of the world, we got the world we deserved, don't you think?

JULIA Maybe you did, but I don't.

JUDD I don't deserve the world I got, but most of us, yeah, uh-huh.

JULIA Well, I've been so blind, so Pollyannaish, so geeky, ah, I smell of science club, don't I? (*Smiling.*) I should give up. I'd been struggling. So. Thank you for helping me decide. I had been struggling with this . . . you know . . . very earnest and boring *idealism*. My enthusiasm. It kept bugging me. And of course it's not attractive to men.

JUDD (*To Fabricant and Raphe.*) Now . . . Why don't we ever have these kinds of talks? Huh? About art and passion and life or death. I would like to have . . . a real conversation now and then.

They laugh. It's easy.

JULIA (*Going on.*) Not knowing precisely when to throw in the towel in the face of a problem as thorny as ecological catastrophe—believe me, I'm in on the joke.

RAPHELSON   I'm not telling you not to *fight* . . . I'm asking how?

JUDD   Yeah. How *do* you fight it?

JULIA   (*She turns her attention to Malcolm. The temperature has shifted within her, and what was light is subtly now not so light.*)   How? Not by smirking certainly. Yeah. And I recognize the smirk. And PS, I don't believe it. I should, but I don't.

Silence. Malcolm nods, somewhat abashed, and gives a gesture of gentle surrender.

RAPHELSON   I hope you don't think I'm trying to offend you.

JULIA   (*Gently. Firmly.*)   Oh. No. I hope you don't think I'm offended . . . ?

RAPHELSON   Because all I'm saying is be careful. Mexico can be rough on the . . . appearance of presumption.

JULIA   Don't worry about me, and I'll keep an eye out for the "appearance of presumption."

She smiles.

FABRICANT   But it's difficult, isn't it, to be passionate about something which is—perhaps a lost cause. Yes, it is, I know all about this, because you see, what I am trying to do with this man here—is redress the "historical editing" which has almost obliterated him.

RAPHELSON   (*Holding up a hand. A warning gesture, calm but serious.*)   Oh let's not start that shit again, son.

FABRICANT   Yes, it's relevant, the draconian historical editing out of someone.

JULIA   Historical editing?

FABRICANT   The process, almost accidental, whereby someone . . . is cut away, untethered from what happened, is left out of the narrative.

RAPHELSON   Oh Trevor, why not shut up, that would be so much better . . .

JUDD   Malcolm here was sorta fucked over by abstract expressionism. (*Beat.*)   They were considered bolder. Braver, truer to their moment.. Yeah. So you can count on one hand pretty much—the figurative painters—who made it through that time. They were cast out by Pollock and his homies.

RAPHELSON   And if you suggested that those guys were hiding behind a mock freedom, made up of decorative fields of color, restaurant painting—really, if you dared to suggest that they were in fact the fretful, tentative, noncommittal conservative ones—you were dead.

JULIA   Like the frogs of Lake Grijalva?

RAPHELSON   Yep. Swallowed whole by a bigmouth bass from Texas, you are a very clever girl, how sad that I'm three hundred times older than you. (*Beat.*)   Yeah. Trevor. You may take back a painting. One of these new ones. But only on one condition: Julia Bryant here gets to select it. She chooses.

JULIA   (*Laughing.*)   Hey, what? Don't drag me in. Hey. No, Julia Bryant does not *select* . . .

JUDD   Yeah, why don't we sorta just have a big old giveaway, right, go around the house and everyone can just take shit.

RAPHELSON   This may be funny to you guys but I'm serious. Julia. I can see you have an eye for the truth, you're not a flatterer or a seducer or a diplomat, so . . .

JULIA   Nevertheless.

RAPHELSON   Make a choice for me, please, consider it a favor.

JULIA   I don't know anything about art, I don't know the criteria.

JUDD   This is not a handicap that has stopped anyone in the past.

RAPHELSON   Fun. A parlor game.

JUDD   Like charades?

FABRICANT   (*Raising an arm.*)   Excuse me please. Hello?

JULIA   (*Laughing.*)   We don't know each other—you expect me to select a painting for this man to sell?

She smiles at Trevor.

RAPHELSON   Yep. It's the only way I'll let him have a canvas.

FABRICANT   (*Trying to control a situation which is spinning out of his grasp.*)   Yes, hah-hah. Very funny. As . . . *curious* . . . and as . . . *entertained* as I am—and I am both curious *and* entertained, I don't feel comfortable abdicating my—

RAPHELSON   I don't care, son. You have no say in the matter.

JULIA   But Malcolm.

RAPHELSON   (*Cuts her off.*)   You'd be doing me a huge service, because these two ghouls have turned me upside down, I don't know what's what. And I'm sorry I've put you on the spot.

JULIA It's my San Francisco propriety. I'm still occasionally a prisoner of what's appropriate.

RAPHELSON Let that go here.

JUDD Why does she get to choose?

RAPHELSON She's a believer. We have to have a believer choose.

There is a moment.

JULIA (*Deciding, nods.*) A believer? (*Beat, she laughs.*) God, that's so lame. Okay then.

RAPHELSON Judd. Please.

Judd takes a large canvas out of the rack. A landscape. Virtually abstract, a sulfuric and apocalyptic lake under a smouldering, clouded desert sky. As much crater as lake. Julia stands before it, stunned, as does Trevor, who is also seeing it for the first time.

JULIA Christ.

FABRICANT The size is right.

JUDD Such a size queen, Trevor.

FABRICANT What exactly do you mean by "Christ"?

JULIA It's Lake Grijalva.

RAPHELSON (*Only looking at Julia, not the painting. He doesn't want or need to see it.*) Is it? Not the lake as we know it. I see that lake, the way it changes constantly, and darkens, bursts into light, light colliding with the dark, but never happily, always at war. Yeah, over and over. Turner did it, this sense of a theology somewhere. Landscapes are never just landscapes. If they work, it's because they're so many other things.

JULIA   Yes. When I'm out there, I know it's—predatory in some way, and I know anything could happen.

FABRICANT   Yes, a dire . . . body of water, eh? Chilling, one thinks of Dante's *Inferno,* of *Moby-Dick,* of Conrad—Kurtz lurking in—

RAPHELSON   (*Cuts Fabricant off.*)   No bullshit in this room, please. (*Back to Julia.*)   You see the little fishing boats? They're like scars. People disappear into that lake. It's a sacrificial pit to me. And then you think back to the Aztecs. Horrifying marvelous people, nothing excited them as much as human sacrifice. See, there's a little smudge in the top corner . . . black . . . ?

JULIA   Yes.

RAPHELSON   The church on the edge of the lake there, it's—Cortés and them folk; wherever there had been a temple, they'd raze it and put up a goddamn church. You think frogs are the only thing that ends up extinct? This whole nation is built on extinction, and extermination, it's all over the place and you can't fight it.

JULIA   You live here, and you love the place, you took me around town today, and you clearly love it, so what do you mean "you can't fight it"? You don't think this . . . qualifies in some way? The smudge, the church, the darkness of the church . . . ? You mentioned a theology? You know more on the subject of extinction than I do. I

22

think that there's some . . . aspiration in the spire, in that smudge . . . ?

RAPHELSON (*Quietly.*)   Very little.

FABRICANT   Yes well, I can't wait to take this up with me, because it proves many points, first of all that this transition into a contemporary idiom, this magnificent redefinition now has the command of an El Greco, a Zuberan. The wall power is off the charts.

RAPHELSON   Trevor. I don't know that I want to let it go. Selling the new work . . . ? I don't know. I'm uneasy, it came hard and it's not . . . (*To Julia.*)   So what do you think? To go or not to go?

JULIA   I wouldn't want to give the appearance of presumption. To know where you're really fucking coming from. I would think I'd need to know you much better before knowing that.

RAPHELSON (*Grinning.*)   Julia. I wanted to show you, I have these sort of amazing cacti in the garden, they're giant and they're unruly, it's like the moon out there, I wanted to show you before it's too dark . . .

JULIA   Yes, sure.

They start to exit.

FABRICANT (*Frustrated, and perhaps furious.*)   Just a second, please, this—toying with me—is—this can't be an entirely capricious endeavor, with me flying down here, a joke.

RAPHELSON   Only if you want it to be, Trevor.

To Julia, as he walks her out.

I'll be out in a sec, you go. There's no reason for anyone to be subjected to this mercantile art biz crap. Let me show you the path, it's hard to spot.

He exits with her.

JUDD Listen. I'm not big on like, "advice" but—Be careful, Trev. I don't think pushing is gonna work.

FABRICANT (*Vigorous and outraged.*) For God's sake. This wrestling match with him, it's farcical, it's actually like boarding school, and I'm not in some eighteenth century courtship with a—the coyness—it's—

Raphelson has returned. He is smiling, languid.

RAPHELSON (*Genial.*) You think this thing was easy to toss off, son?

FABRICANT (*Calm.*) Not at all.

RAPHELSON (*A whisper. He comes very close to Fabricant, is not looking at him.*) Yes, it's not. Because things do not want to be painted. Do you understand, things do not want to be seen. Not by me at least, shapes retreat from me and disappear and so getting it close to where you want it . . .

FABRICANT It is quite clear from this painting who won this battle.

RAPHELSON (*A nod.*) All right then. I'm disappointing you.

FABRICANT No.

RAPHELSON (*Still sweet, still quiet, still pleasant. He lights a cigarette, offers one to Fabricant.*) Okay then. Good. Trevor. It's good to know. (*With even more patience and kindly menace.*) Then—Don't you fucking dare ever again, to speak to me, like I'm some kaffir on your daddy's vineyard outside Cape Town. Okay? I'm not a shiftless subcontractor who didn't deliver the zinfandel, and I'm not a child, and there will be respect here in this room, or you won't *be* in this room. You can walk away or you can be patient and mannerly and don't rush me. There's nothing you have to offer that I need. Got it? I like you, but I don't need you.

Malcolm starts to exit.

FABRICANT (*Dignified and straight ahead.*)   Malcolm. Forgive me. You see the very worst of me. Wanting what I want when I want it. Sheer manic greed on my part. But please understand: If I didn't respect you, do you think I would do this?

RAPHELSON (*A shrug.*)   I dunno. I once knew a girl in Beverly Hills who liked to defecate on lovers, but only those she regarded highly. She was a good lay and that was supposed to be a compliment. (*Beat.*)   I passed.

To Judd, who can no longer suppress his giggles. Raphe is grinning.

RAPHELSON (*cont.*)   See, kid? Art can make people behave very badly if it's got somethin' goin' on. It's a good sign. Very good.

He pats Judd's shoulder and exits. Judd, still laughing, takes a joint out of a tin and lights it.

FABRICANT   When I offered you this job, you assured me, did you not, that you would adhere to strict rules of behavior which I can see are being flagrantly ignored.

JUDD (*Laughing.*)   What the hell are you talkin' about? "Flagrantly ignored," what is this—*Lord of the Flies* or something?

FABRICANT (*Growing angrier, continuing his thought, all with a veneer of civility, but not at all convivial.*)   For instance, I

25

heard a little short, sharp snort of *laughter* when I mentioned a New York showing. "It's not MOMA." And I thought to myself, "Judd? . . A question for later is: Why on earth, did you not back me up"?

He shrugs, wanting an answer.

FABRICANT (*cont.*)   As entertaining as this circus is to you, I think it might be useful for you to occasionally remember what you've been afforded, Judd.

JUDD   Remind me.

FABRICANT (*Dead on, ice cold.*)   You've been afforded the opportunity not to be a nasty little Gotham arriviste who only quite recently was operating the prosciutto machine at Dean and DeLuca.

JUDD   And you, Trev, get to graduate from third-tier gallerist trying to get in on shit early to actually being like— relevant, if you don't persist in saying the wrong thing at the exactly wrong moment.

FABRICANT   Does he hate me?

JUDD   Oh. He should, but he doesn't.

FABRICANT   I think I am getting sick, I feel all white and clammy. This is a nightmare. It's turned into an actual nightmare, I get sick here, that's the end. A vomiting art dealer, sprawled on the bathroom floor is not persuasive.

JUDD   Oh I dunno. Tell me about New York. What am I missing?

FABRICANT   It's the same. It's reputations made based on mirage tricks at watering holes. Yes, the only thing I liked at the Whitney Biennial was they gave out little buttons which essentially said "white people are assholes."

JUDD   You see what you're making me miss?

FABRICANT   The girl. She could be good for his work. It might get him to speed up and all. This friendship. So, if you could find some way to not be a complete ponce with her?

Judd nods and hands Trevor the joint. Trevor indulges.

JUDD   I like her. I hope he's fuckin' her in the cactus garden as we speak.

FABRICANT   And while you know I enjoy being in the orbit of this smirking and goading mode of discourse you seem to employ with Raphelson, I do think it's dangerous. It could topple over and get out of hand.

JUDD   It could. You're right.

FABRICANT   You no doubt think I am being too micro-managerial and fussy. I know that when you disagree, your strategy is to NOT argue at all.

JUDD   As my employer, it's your responsibility to try and correct the areas where my performance could be better. I appreciate it. I want to be a better assistant. I'm trying. I really am. I want to, I want to. I want to. I know I can if I try real hard.

FABRICANT   Judd, we have to be able to talk openly.

JUDD   (*Now eager to strike back.*)   Yeah? What as? Ex-boyfriends? Work buddies? Employee and baas? When the South African landowner comes out in you, that's when I know there's a problem. The accent is the giveaway. It becomes a little more imperious and British. And there's this regretful "I hate to tell you, but you don't measure up, do you?' tone which I'm

sure knocked 'em dead in Cape Town, where you were . . .
spawned . . . but it doesn't do much for me.

FABRICANT   This is the precise difficulty of friends working
together.

JUDD   (*Over him.*)   Look. Look at the new work. One of
Rafe's wives.

*Judd takes a painting off the rack, making sure Raphe is not returning
first. A large nude of a woman holding a sweater.*

JUDD   (*cont.*)   Look at the hand. The surety. You have no idea
how hard it is to create that sleight of hand.

FABRICANT   (*Transfixed.*)   It's riveting. Yes. I will admit.

JUDD   This is a man who was stuck in a calcified language.
Have you noticed the colors in that lake picture? They
shouldn't work, and they do, because it's come back to
him, and you found him and fucking trust the process a
little. And let us do our work!

FABRICANT   Yes.

JUDD   However he wants to, at whatever pace. And as for the
"mode of discourse" between him and me, let me tell you:
It works. Macho banter and sparring. He doesn't want
sweet. He wants what I am, whatever I am . . . I don't
really know.

FABRICANT   No, I can see you do seem to have formed a
somewhat bizarre special attachment.

JUDD   (*Delighted.*)   Hey, are you like jealous?

FABRICANT   I think what I'm trying to say, is that this . . .
new Judd—"Mexico Judd," shall we call him?—this
arrogant and rather insouciant Judd is not my Judd.

JUDD Were I some hectoring little queer outta Chelsea, he'd have booted me on day three.

FABRICANT And of course he's one of those old lefty Bohemian artists who are smugly repulsed by homosexuals.

JUDD Only shifty greasy ones like you.

FABRICANT No, no. I know the type. (*Thanks, by the way. Greasy am I?*) No, I can tell his type. They find homosexuals slightly off-putting unless they're outrageous and flamboyantly epicene like Oscar Wilde or Truman Capote.

JUDD (*Grinning.*) I got news for you: You are *exactly* like Oscar Wilde and Truman Capote. You're practically their godchild.

Fabricant raises his eyebrows and with deliberate self-mocking theatricality takes out a handkerchief and wipes his brow.

FABRICANT I have *no* idea what you're talking about.

This is easy; they are both now having fun. There is a moment. Judd shakes his head.

JUDD You make me laugh. Man, you make me laugh, you leave nothing to chance. I mean: You seek this man out. You track down the most obscure drunk, broken old guy in Mexico, you plot a course, and you leave nothing to chance.

FABRICANT (*Seriously.*) This is my nature, Judd. This is my training.

JUDD The only chance you took was on me. And I am grateful, you picked me up outta the sewer, practically. I mean it.

Beat. A gentle inquiry.

JUDD (*cont.*)   Is that what you needed to hear?

Judd kisses Trevor. The moment of it extends itself, and for Fabricant it is quite hungry. Judd pulls away.

FABRICANT (*Staring at Judd. Quietly.*)   Christ. Just because I'm still slightly, and I mean slightly—you know—fucked up about you—doesn't mean—

JUDD   No it doesn't—What do you mean by you're still fucked up about me?

FABRICANT   I'm not like you, Judd. I'm practically forty, I have no actual talent except for a decent eye, and it's been a rare day when I'm in the right place at the right time. But right now, I might be. People are in a panic. The bottom has dropped out of the market, the Neiki's evaporated, and filthy broken plates on canvas are finally worthless. People are longing for authenticity, and suddenly an artist materializes out of the mists of the WPA and he fits the bill perfectly.

Beat.

FABRICANT (*cont.*)   We have, *I* have—stumbled into something very good, you see, with this artist. And I actually like him. I find it easy to respect him without too much looking the other way.

JUDD   Me too.

FABRICANT   And there are moments for certain ideas, styles in any culture. And in a culture as reactionary and as staggeringly backward looking as American culture circa 1992, the word of the day is nostalgia. Nostalgia is everything.

JUDD You make it sound so calculated.

FABRICANT Yes. Does that make you squeamish?

JUDD He's actually good.

FABRICANT (*Nodding.*) Yes. And it almost never happens that way. And he's better since you've been here. However . . . I must acknowledge a growing awareness that a large part of this job involves drinking.

JUDD Here we go.

Judd moans and rolls his eyes.

FABRICANT You can moan all you like, but you must admit, you've hardly been the guardian of your modest gifts.

JUDD (*Mock outrage.*) Modest? Modest?

FABRICANT Well I mean, come on, please admit that you are a past-master in squandered gifts. I mean—heroin, ecstasy, showpeople . . . the list . . .

He gestures to show how long the list is.

FABRICANT (*cont.*) I mean, it's long . . .

JUDD (*Laughing, shaking his head.*) Always keeping accounts, Trevor, it's so fucking joyless.

FABRICANT The list goes on, and you've nothing to show for it except anemia, depression, and eviction notices. He's my only shot. I need your help in handling this man; this is your job!

JUDD You have those old pictures of his, from the old days, just sell them for now, and let him—

FABRICANT (*Cuts him off.*) I've spent the last bloody year rooting in attics in Scranton, Pennsylvania, fishing out molding Raphelsons, and I've got a baker's dozen—just enough—

Beat.

FABRICANT (*cont.*)   Judd, you don't understand. The Bernard Kruger Gallery has given me three rooms to show Raphelson. A retrospective. 1942 . . . (*He takes in the rack of new work.*)   To 1992. I've got about six weeks to move all this stuff up there.

Judd says nothing.

FABRICANT (*cont.*)   What? What?

JUDD   You took a big-ass gallery? You made this deal? Already? He didn't agree to a fucking—you know—a *retrospective*, man.

Fabricant shrugs. Finally Judd shakes his head, thinking.

JUDD (*cont.*)   And you want to know what else? He's not ready.

FABRICANT   Really? You think? Why do you say that?

JUDD   He has to decide for himself, not you and your coercive—whispering down the lane—he has to decide for sure . . .

FABRICANT (*Curious.*)   . . . And *you* are in a position to determine this?

Gently.

FABRICANT (*cont.*)   Judd. There is a great deal of *money* involved in this business, some of which will go to you. Wipe out your debts, start anew, earn the way out of the hole you are in.

JUDD   I thought I already had. I thought I was doing well down here.

FABRICANT   Not five minutes ago you just argued for the value of his new work. So—*Why* is he not ready? He's become *good* again. It is urgent that we get him out there now, because it would be kind—of nice if he were actually— *(Suddenly impassioned.)*   Still fucking . . . *alive* to experience this vindication! Do you not want to witness this?

JUDD   New York is a tough town and the Kruger Gallery is on 57th Street, right? Unleashing him there could fuck up the rest of his life, if they do what they did to him fifty years ago.

Fabricant starts to answer but Raphelson enters with Julia in tow.

RAPHELSON   This woman here has been living in mortal danger.

JULIA *(Amused.)*   No, squalor, mortal *squalor*—

RAPHELSON *(Overriding her.)*   Yes, that too. There was a shotgun blast, her dinghy.

JUDD   That can't be good.

JULIA   I wasn't anywhere near it. It was a warning, it was almost respectful.

RAPHELSON   Yes, *this time*, but you don't want it to go further. We're sitting here with all this space. I'm well liked here, that you were under my roof would be noted. I can't offer much. As I said. But this I can do.

Beat. Julia is nodding, thinking, trying to make a decision. Raphe sees this process at work. Quietly goes on. He is letting himself be vulnerable.

33

RAPHELSON (*cont.*)   When I was starting out, when I was living in East L.A. there were these dinners, painters—Phil Guston, Diebenkorn, Park—me, these guys—women, always women and the cheapest red wine you could get, and a big pot of spaghetti, and up all night fighting and talking . . . so much to talk about.

JUDD   But more to fight about, right?

FABRICANT   Yes, the bonhomie, dinners en famille. The lost art of conversation, of table talk.

RAPHELSON (*Beat, quizzical.*)   Uhm. Tell me you talk in that ridiculous manner for comic effect please, son.

FABRICANT (*Taking a moment to consider, nodding.*)   . . . Mostly, yes.

RAPHELSON (*To Julia.*)   I'm saying I miss talk, I miss people.

JUDD   And now that you have so much to say . . .

RAPHELSON   So of course you boys don't mind sharing a room—do you?

FABRICANT   Not at all.

RAPHELSON   And Judd doesn't mind you shacking up with him while you're here, Trevor, so then, Julia: The guest room is now no longer a guest room—it is your room.

JUDD   There you go, problem solved.

RAPHELSON (*A sly shrug.*)   And I know you two boys are "special friends," you were looking forward to having Trevor visit, Judd, it was almost cute, cleaning, cutting flowers and shit, it was kinda like a lost love comin' back from years at sea.

JUDD   Not love, Mal, just fucking, that's all.

He playfully slaps Fabricant's ass.

FABRICANT (*Almost a whisper but serious to Judd, through his smile at the others.*) Stop!

To Raphelson and Julia.

FABRICANT (*cont.*) This is great, please, I'm very happy to oblige, let me gather my stuff and tidy up in there and . . .

He starts out.

JULIA Hey, are you all sure—it's *so* generous and—

JUDD (*Cuts her off.*) There's room for all at the Casa del Art.

JULIA Is there a phone . . . ? I would love to be able to—

RAPHELSON I'm sorry, it's something I never needed.

FABRICANT If you'd had one, I wouldn't have had to schlepp down here, would I?

He exits.

RAPHELSON Judd. You know, we were talking about the little bit of neon we saw at the butcher's . . . where it was broken . . . ?

JUDD The ochre . . . ? That was more mocha than red . . . ?

RAPHELSON Exactly. Do you think you could mix that up?

JUDD (*Surprised.*) Yeah . . . (*Beat.*) Now?

RAPHELSON (*Nodding, staring at Judd, not particularly with much patience.*) *Right now* actually. I want to get to work. (*He smiles at Julia.*) There's a fireplace in your room, and I have some very good wood for it, I'll put it in there for you . . . (*He studies her.*) You have almost *good* bones, you know.

He exits.

JUDD (*After a moment.*)   Good bones. That's . . . He may want to paint you.

Judd sets about mixing paints for Raphe.

JULIA   And I was just getting used to the weirdness of my little shack on the lake.

JUDD   Now you don't have to. It's good here. It's warm and fun and dry pretty much. You have some self-defense skills, don't you?

JULIA   Will they be required for some reason?

JUDD   You think people give up lust at a certain point? Picasso, he was like, impotent and all at the end, and he was feelin' up whoever came into his orbit.

JULIA   Uh-huh. Okay.

JUDD   The price of a room is eternal vigilance.

JULIA   Great.

JUDD   Here.

He tosses her a piece of Mexican chocolate.

JUDD (*cont.*)   Oaxacan chocolate; lots of caffeine and cinnamon, keep you alert.

JULIA   No. He's attractive, he's charming and charismatic. I can see how one might want to . . .

JUDD (*Laughing.*)   Yeah. One might. Holy fuck, you are so doomed.

JULIA   Point taken? Maybe I should just stay where I am?

JUDD   You travelled much?

JULIA (*Nodding.*)   It's what I do. Why'd he leave the States? He makes it sound like a door closed and he kept walking.

JUDD   He got in that old pickup truck outside, and he drove down here. Yeah.

JULIA But the idealism and the politics. They're gone?

JUDD   He believes in beauty and shit; art's power to be a force for good. He'd painted this mural in Bakersfield at some post office, I think it was painted over in '54 . . . Trotsky or someone was apparently like, you know, delivering the mail in it in the left hand corner . . . so . . .

JULIA I see.

JUDD   I know you come from Berkeley and maybe this is news to you but not everyone has "politics."

JULIA Oh. No, right, I mean, yes . . . I can see that.

JUDD   Here it's sort of about just getting by pretty much. This is sorta . . . where the demons seem to like to hang out.

JULIA Fair enough. (*Beat. A moment.*)   But what's your deal? Why are you here? Because you seem like the last word in urban boy to me.

JUDD   (*Laughing, liking that.*)   I *am,* I am *the* last word in "urban boy"—What do you *mean* by that?

JULIA Smart, spoilt, and coasting.

JUDD   That's good, 'cause I'd hate to have made a bad impression.

Beat.

JUDD   (*cont.*)   "Why am I here?" This—here—is work. My work. A steady paycheck. And a kind of informal detox before tackling the big world up north again. I'm using it as an opportunity offered by my dear pal Trevor.

JULIA   That's so nice of him. An opportunity . . . For . . . ?

JUDD   A rigorous and very monastic examination of the dangers of American life.

JULIA   Got it. Such as . . . ?

JUDD   (*Smiling.*)   Oh. Pretty much everything you've apparently effortlessly concluded about me. You know. The usual stuff.

She smiles back.

JUDD   (*cont.*)   Sedatives, stimulants, sex clubs, money, dirty sex . . . stayin' out all night . . .

JULIA   Right. Probably it's good to take a break from those things sometimes, sure.

JUDD   And reflect on them.

JULIA   . . . From a safe and irony-free distance?

JUDD   You got it.

There is silence.

JUDD   (*cont.*)   What?

JULIA   (*Shaking her head. Quietly, staring at him.*)   You remind me of someone.

JUDD   Do I? Who? I can guess: someone totally disgusting you met once at some party you were slumming at, is that it? Or like—*The Fly* . . .

She shakes her head, smiling.

38

JULIA So. You're here because it's business. A job, a paycheck, a transaction, right? And we know—In all such deals, someone gets the short end of the stick.

Judd looks at her, shaking his head, and crosses his arms.

JUDD (*Grinning.*) And who might that be?

JULIA I'm not saying—

JUDD (*Gently over her.*) Not everything is what it seems. Don't they teach you guys that at *frog school*?

JULIA (*She takes the point graciously.*) I'm just saying that it's complicated, isn't it? I mean, I can't help but notice that there's this thing, this tussle—between you two and . . . like he doesn't *want* to sell his work or . . . ? And Fabricant is . . . Well . . .

Judd shrugs, nods.

JUDD There is this "thing." (*Beat.*) This "tussle."

Beat. She is nodding. It does not mollify him. Suddenly he is dark as Raphe, it's a shot, but it's returning fire and not vicious, just dead on target . . .

JUDD (*cont.*) With all due respect, and I might be really off base here, but you seem awfully gung ho for the snappy judgements? Is that unfair of me?

JULIA (*Not really all that apologetic.*) No, it's not unfair. I do that, I try not to. I apologize.

JUDD You don't have to. (*Beat.*) It's hard to have an assistant when you've been doin' it alone forever, and it's hard to *be* an assistant if you've never been one and aren't built for it, and if you think I'm here under false pretenses, you go, girl; doesn't bother me.

She nods, not convinced. Judd sighs. Looking at her.

RAPHELSON (*Entering.*)   I lit a fire in your room, dear. The wood has a palliative effect, if you can't sleep.

Beat. He sees the residual of whatever just passed.

RAPHELSON (*cont.*)   Are you spreading lies about me, boy? Julia, he's Pinocchio, you can't believe a word he says.

JULIA   Orientation, is all. I guess I should go down to the lake and get some stuff.

RAPHELSON   Oh no, no, tomorrow—you don't want to go back and forth again. There's a brand-new toothbrush in the hall closet . . .

JULIA   Thanks, I'm actually exhausted and dirty, and all. God, you have a shower and hot water . . . ?

RAPHELSON   Often.

JULIA (*Kissing him on the cheek.*)   At last. Thanks. I have to get to the lake early. I set traps.

JUDD   I'm sure.

She leaves. Silence.

RAPHELSON   She's all the things I missed and forced out of my head, you know? The smart, sexy American girl who doesn't have to be nice. I thought they were extinct.

JUDD   You've been away for a long time, pal.

RAPHELSON   It's the only thing I gave up that I . . .

JUDD   Never too late for all that stuff.

RAPHELSON   Right. Never too late to be pole-axed all of a sudden. (*Beat.*)   So let's get to work.

JUDD (*Bemused.*)   . . . Okay. You have something . . . in mind . . . ?

RAPHELSON (*Looking for something.*)   Yeah. My mom. Yeah. (*He finds an old photograph.*)   Here she is. This tough and totally inelegant Russian broad. But very delicate. This girl, she's got the same . . . it's temperature, she's reminding me—of the things I liked about my mother. Came to America with nothing. The way those people did. Got on those fucking boats without the vaguest sense of what was awaiting them.

JUDD   . . . Okay.

Judd places a large canvas on the easel. He looks at the photograph and then at Raphelson.

JUDD (*cont.*)   So this is the size canvas . . . ? Or there's some smaller ones I stretched today, they're in the . . .

RAPHELSON (*Cuts him off.*)   Yeah. She had these hands, they were so private, they were . . . you didn't want to look at them.

Judd nods. Raphe smiles. Looks at him, laughing.

RAPHELSON (*cont.*)   You don't understand, do you? The poverty. The starvation rations. Piecemeal work, you don't know what that is, do you? Then—opening a fucking *hat store* in Boyle Heights on First Avenue. Women's hats.

JUDD   You've never worked at night before.

RAPHELSON   Oh, I have. You think when I was talkin' and drinkin' I was playin' around? It's hard work, waiting for something to come into focus. *That's work*, now it's almost—anticlimactic.

Raphe hands Judd the photograph of his mother.

RAPHELSON (*cont.*)   Bcause now I can see her face, and it's the face of someone who wants to love you, it is fierce and also so angry. Beautiful, beautiful eyes and so many fucking secrets in there. (*He lights a smoke.*)   She was half mad.

JUDD   That's something I understand.

RAPHELSON   The thing is this. Boys. They get one thing from their mothers, never comes from fathers. Maybe later that happens but boys are so scared when they are little, and they only really trust the mom, and if she can live up to it— They get courage from the women in their lives.

JUDD   My mom was on another plan; the "life's dangerous" one, where you're taught that germs and cars and cats are only here to mow you down and kill you—

RAPHELSON (*Bored with Judd's futile attempt at profundity.*)   Yeah.

Raphe examines the paint Judd has mixed. He picks up a brush, thinking. Nodding. Staring at the canvas.

JUDD   You want music?

RAPHELSON   Bill Evans maybe or there's a Mose Allison.

Uninterested.

RAPHELSON (*cont.*)   . . . Whatever . . .

Judd puts an album on the old turntable. Raphelson nods. He tries to hit the canvas lightly with the brush, but steps back.

RAPHELSON (*cont.*)   Public pools. She loved public pools. That green tile, the diving board, and men staring at her.

He steps away, shaking his head, staring at the canvas. The following are a series of spontaneous discoveries.

RAPHELSON (*cont.*)   The Boyle Heights Pool. She's in front of it, older maybe but . . . yes . . . she's—the powers are waning, the sex magic is now slightly . . . grotesque.

JUDD   She's in front of the . . . ?

RAPHELSON   The Boyle Heights Pool. East L.A. So good, to feel like, after all the uncertainty, which is like being *color blind,* to have a moment of hope here.

JUDD   Right . . . sure.

Judd studies the photo in his hand. Raphe goes back to the canvas, Judd watches expectantly. Raphe steps back again.

JUDD (*cont.*)   This pool. Is there light on the water?

RAPHELSON   It's jagged. Makes for a counterbalance to the dark. It's almost blinding. White. Little jagged serrations on the water.

JUDD (*Bewildered.*)   Do you—do you remember what color green it was? This little tile?

RAPHELSON   It's grout and putty green gray.

JUDD   The pool? Do we see it all or just like, like a corner, with like maybe the—the—the diving board.

RAPHELSON (*Finally has had it, starts as a slow burn.*)   Forget the fucking pool, it's not about the pool, you fucking moron, it's her! Don't get lost in the fucking architectural detail, it's about where we place her! She's primary!

JUDD   Okay, okay okay—Keep talking, I'm listening.

RAPHELSON   Figure the balance out, the composition out, and worry about the tile work when someone hires you as a goddamn pool attendant's assistant.

Judd simply stands there.

RAPHELSON (*cont.*) You look like a deer in headlights, son; you okay?

JUDD (*Quietly.*) Yeah. This is just different, you're all charged up. Go for it.

RAPHELSON (*Furious.*) Well. That's what I'm doing! What do you think I'm doing here? Telling you a bedtime story?

JUDD It's a matter of defiling the temple, the first mark on a blank canvas, isn't it? You told me that, "defile the temple and tear it down and then cover it in paint" you said.

RAPHELSON Yes. Okay.

JUDD (*Quietly.*) Then fucking defile your temple.

RAPHELSON Yes! (*Points at Judd.*) Okay.

He nods, staring at the canvas. He moves towards it, and the paint is about to make contact.

RAPHELSON (*cont.*) (*Almost to himself.*) It's here. It's a diagonal.

JUDD Yes, right there. Just do it.

RAPHELSON I can't. I'm caught. I'm stuck.

JUDD You're so close.

RAPHELSON I can't. You do it.

JUDD I can't.

RAPHELSON Take the brush for Christ's sake!

JUDD Malcolm. We can't keep doing this.

RAPHELSON I'm just asking you to do some of the lifting in here. Do your goddamn job.

JUDD I should go back home, this is not what you need.

RAPHELSON Take the brush, please.

Judd takes the brush.

RAPHELSON (*cont.*) (*Now berserk.*) Y'know what? I'm not doin' this anymore, it's like fuckin' art therapy with you! You've got to stop being scared of my life—this sickness. (*Beat.*) Let's not lie to each other, kid. Look at you. (*Quietly.*) I think you have some very good techniques and some even better . . . technical . . . instincts, in other words; you gotta good bag of tricks along the way, must've been art school, BUT I would prefer to watch you do some of the . . . (*With quiet ferocity. Great danger.*) . . . fucking *lifting in here*. For a change. Because I sometimes feel like I'm just here to *educate* you to the inner—more mysterious inner mechanics of this process called painting! And I would prefer it if you wouldn't just stare at me, taking in the show, gaping at the goddamn monkey cage, but *rather started this canvas!*

He throws the brush hard and Judd catches it, or picks it up from the floor. Judd walks over to the canvas, looks at it. Raphelson sits down. Judd is about to make a line.

And Judd does. Raphe watches. Judd deals confidently with the most primitive aspects of laying in an outline, and then he falters. He doesn't know what comes next.

RAPHELSON (*cont.*) Yeah, okay. You got tied up, didn't you? It's a diagonal. And it's counter to the way the sun hits the pool, there are grooves in the tile, there are grooves in the wooden bench and the diving board and her face, my mother's.

Judd pauses.

RAPHELSON (*cont.*)   You got tied up didn't you? (*A smile.*)   That's always the question. "What comes next?" Because it's all somewhere, there's a plan, you might have forgotten it, like you forget a dream when you wake up, but it's there.

JUDD   How do you know?

RAPHELSON   You never really do. Look at me. I mean . . .

Raphelson stops. The blackness in this man at this moment is simply unendurable.

RAPHELSON (*cont.*)   (*Quietly menacing.*)   Judd. That color; it's slack. It's not . . . true. Is it?

JUDD (*Terrified.*)   Is it?

RAPHELSON (*Slowly standing like he is going to murder.*)   The truth is, my mother, she was after my balls. Yeah. (*He moves closer to Judd and canvas, stops.*)   She really was a cunt, Sara Raphelson.

He moves towards Judd, who backs away from the worktable.

RAPHELSON (*cont.*)   She made so much trouble and she loved me so much. A monster and then a little kid . . .

Raphe picks up a paint tube, considering it. Squirts some red paint in the palm of his hand during the following, still considering, and still quiet.

RAPHELSON (*cont.*)   First you're not actually not good enough for her, and then you're too good for her. And the trick to painting my mom is . . . BOTH have to be there. The ice cream and the razor blades, or you've got nothing.

He smears red paint onto the canvas with his hand; the paint starts to resemble the atavistic form of a figure. And he turns to Judd.

Lights fade down on the two of them.

The next morning. There has been much work done on the portrait of Sara Raphelson. As much as possible in one long night. Dark tones predominate, and violent, stormy energy seems to tilt the world of the portrait into an angry sorrow. Judd, filthy with paint, which is everywhere, is asleep on the sofa, crumbled into a fetal position, a blanket over him, out to the world, despite Lou Reed (the New York album) blasting on the stereo. Julia enters quietly with a mug of coffee, places it on a table for him, takes in the painting for a moment, and quietly starts to exit.

JUDD I'm up, don't go.

JULIA I heard the music. I have coffee.

Judd sits up and holds the mug.

JUDD Thanks. I'm supposed to be doin' stuff, I keep lying down again.

JULIA He must have been painting all night.

JUDD Yeah, he does this thing, it's like this—witches' brew of tequila, eggs, coffee, and these little nasty cigarettes that he only smokes at three-forty-five a.m.

JULIA And you . . . ?

JUDD Help, clean up, make the eggs, light the smokes, clean messes. You sleep well here?

JULIA That fireplace put me out. (*Taking in the painting.*) Who's she?

JUDD Sara Raphelson. His mother.

JULIA She looks pretty tough.

47

JUDD Yeah. A dark and vengeful Old Testament goddess. But something else too.

JULIA There's . . . a certain sweetness . . . ?

JUDD But it's . . . very tentative. A certain kind of parent.

JULIA Who will let you down in the most terrible ways.

JUDD You try and imagine the best in this woman, and then cover it with—a curse. He has this idea about mothers and sons. They program boys for bravery. But it's hard, and she knows she's not doing it right.

JULIA Inducing fear and rage and forty years of flight into the desert?

JUDD (*Pleased. Quietly.*) I think that's the idea, yes.

There is a moment as they take in the incomplete painting.

JULIA (*Straight on.*) I hope that if he decides to let these go to New York, you all know what you're doing.

JUDD I got down here thinking this was all gonna be cornball nostalgia, sentimentality and Rockwellian—like—social e*arnestness,* you know . . . and now I just . . . can't get away.

JULIA (*Surprised.*) So. You don't want to leave?

JUDD (*A shrug.*) I can't. I mean, what? Leave him to . . . ?

JULIA Yes, I can sense how much he needs you.

JUDD But the rules are constantly changing, and there are all these little battles raging. And my boss, Trev—is very—he's got his plan and get out of his way . . .

JULIA But you're part of these plans, aren't you; this *merchandising* plan, isn't that what it is? To take him and—

JUDD Yeah, you've told me already. Listen, maybe that's actually not why I'm here . . . ? (*Very pointed.*) Possibly.

He stops himself.

JUDD (*cont.*) I went to art school. And this place was built to be like—if the art school didn't "*work out,*" they actually built it so it could be converted in *minute*s to a fuckin' *hospital*, so they were all covering their bets, right? (*Beat.*) And it was essentially a kind of Bohemian post-teen nursery school, a lot of it. Not all. Mostly. Turning out these hordes of scruffy-looking people like me. You didn't even have to be able to draw. At all. Technical . . . skills were smirked at. You could take endless Polaroids of toilets, flushed or not, you could just do thousands of those, for three years, and leave with a little gold star. Some kid got surveillance tapes from Kmart and ran them in a loop. He was the hero of my class. Like some sort of valedictorian. Some other kid moved to New York and recreated—in a gallery in Noho, a little store, the kind inside a car wash, with rows and rows of Turtle Wax and air freshener things . . .

JULIA Yeah, well that sounds, actually, kind of terrific.

JUDD Oh yeah, great. And I thought it was the real thing, the only thing; I was *brainwashed*. (*Beat.*) But I could draw, and I knew what paint could, maybe sometimes, be made to do, but I had no training really. And oftentimes I thought those people making car washes and videos were better off. They had something to say at least, even if it was dull and trite.

JULIA School does that. You have your self erased and then you have to go find it elsewhere, don't you?

JUDD Where?

JULIA I don't know. Authenticity is generally not to be found in the academy, Judd. Nobody I studied with actually let me get close. I learned more being alone in the field than I ever did in the lab.

JUDD Exactly.

Staring her down, and no longer Judd the slacker.

JULIA (*Blinking, embarrassed.*) Right . . . I—I really didn't mean—

JUDD (*Cuts her off.*) We don't know each other, you know, but you're truly welcome here, we could even be almost friends, what I'm saying is: Forget schemes and stuff, forget Fabricant and money. You're right. I am taking something from Raphe. He definitely has something to give me, something I've never seen before, something compelling, okay? And I will take that.

There is a moment. Judd just looks at her. She gets it. I think it's that moment, for Julia, when you begin to realize how you've quite possibly made very serious miscalculations, and are slightly ashamed, and also relieved to have been wrong. Raphelson enters.

JULIA Good morning.

JUDD (*Cheery, casual.*) Hey. What's up, Raphe?

RAPHELSON (*To Julia.*) You slept well, and you've already been to the lake?

JULIA Yes to both. So comfortable. And now fully I understand not leaving this spot for twenty-eight years. The smell of those—what—night-blooming jasmine . . . ? and what else . . . eucalyptus. And . . . something else . . . ?

RAPHELSON Jacaranda. It's this perfume, Year-round. So, Judd, you get some rest too?

JUDD   Sorta. I fell asleep in here.

RAPHELSON   Frogs?

JULIA   I don't expect to. This morning, out there, I thought, "This is turning into a vigil . . . "

RAPHELSON   Of course you know, the hardest thing is to keep going. Not giving up.

JUDD   That can be a bitch, for sure.

RAPHELSON   (*An odd look on his face, still looking at the painting.*) You guys want to walk into town? (*To Judd.*)   She doesn't know the little *panadería* by the cemetery—you know . . . ? (*To Julia.*)   Terrible bakers, except for one little sweet tiny roll they do. One little roll has kept them in business for thirty years.

JULIA   Yes, sure.

JUDD   Good idea.

Raphelson walks up to the painting.

RAPHELSON   How'd I let that happen? The hands aren't right.

JUDD   The hands.

RAPHELSON   Of course, hands. Look at Julia's hands. Strong, sure of themselves, and trembling.

JULIA   (*Smiling.*)   There's no *trembling.* I don't think . . .

RAPHELSON   It's hidden but hands give away secrets.

JUDD   (*Looking at his hands.*)   It's just one lesson after the other here.

He puts his hands in his pocket. Trevor Fabricant has entered, unnoticed, standing in doorway.

51

RAPHELSON (*Picks up a rag and starts wiping away paint. Judd turns away, goes to clean a brush.*)   And *these* hands suggest that her secret is . . . cabbage.

JUDD (*Lightly, recovered.*)   That can't be good.

RAPHELSON   If you like veggies it is. *What* was I doing?

JUDD   Rhetorical question, right? You want me to get rid of the cabbages . . . ?

To Julia.

JUDD (*cont.*)   In the morning light, you see all the . . . mistakes . . .

RAPHELSON (*He is rubbing at the canvas, quite hard. Concentrating.*)   I'm doin' it. That's the thing, the thing you get to do . . . go back and clean up . . . and *fix* and, then start over. (*Julia is baffled at the undertones of punishment from Raphe.*)

JUDD   Just like real life.

JULIA   Do you want to go into town another time?

RAPHELSON (*Turns to her.*)   No, no, come on, let's all walk down the hill, a little walk, show Julia around some more, introduce her, put on a little show.

JUDD (*Smiling. But very cool.*)   I think I'm going to maybe pass on the "little rolls at the little place that only has *one* trick," I'm feeling a little . . . sick.

RAPHELSON   Okay. (*To Julia.*)   I think my mode of working is taking a toll on him, but the fact is, he's got to adjust to me.

FABRICANT (*Making himself known.*)   Morning. Hi. Julia hello. Malcolm.

JULIA   Hello. (*Beat.*)   I'm ready whenever. I'll be outside.

She exits.

RAPHELSON   Trevor. You slept well . . . ?

FABRICANT   Malcolm. I see what's going on here. Judd—
sorry, but, Mal—You want another assistant, I shall send
someone else down, clearly you and Judd are—

RAPHELSON   (*Cuts him off, laughing.*)   No, no, no, no. Trevor.
We're great, this is how it works, assistants tire. It's always
been that, they get tired, because they can't control it,
anybody else you send would be exactly the same.

He is studying the incomplete picture.

FABRICANT   (*Quietly, in a kind of reverie.*)   You must let me
. . . do what I do, with this very large and dangerous-
looking picture, Mr. Raphelson, you simply must, when
you're satisfied with her hands and everything else, let me
take this to New York and make your life better.

RAPHELSON   Yep, that's the pitch. "New York will save you.
And New York will—"

FABRICANT   (*Politely.*)   Why don't you actually shut up for a
moment. You are giving rather short shrift to the value of
vengeance.

RAPHELSON   Vengeance, huh?

FABRICANT   Because I, for one, want them *all* to get down
on their knobbly little bifocaled pudgy little white knees
and say "Sorry, we were wrong. This man is better than we
are, this man is superior, and we are deeply humbled and
deeply flawed."

RAPHELSON   All right, enough. Look, Judd, would you leave
Trevor and me alone for a while, I'm not comfortable
having this discussion about New York in front of you—

JUDD   I'm—I'm part of this. You expect me to carry your bags and to—

RAPHELSON   You are involved, as my assistant. Please . . .

He gestures toward the door. Judd does not know what to say to this. He exits. There is a moment.

FABRICANT   You think I'm a joke, which is fine. God knows. But there's something you don't know about me. I had a little trouble with the law. I spray-painted over a Carpaccio painting in The Prado eighteen years ago.

There is silence. Raphelson looks at Fabricant, not sure what to make of this.

RAPHELSON   (*He laughs.*)   Vittore Carpaccio? The Venetian painter? The guy who did boats and monkeys and shit like that? (*Beat. He thinks.*)   You're—you're that guy? The art student . . . ?

FABRICANT   Exactly.

RAPHELSON   I remember . . . tell me what happened . . . ?

FABRICANT   Carpaccio, born around 1455, died maybe 1525, and the monkey and boats and flags flying and life bustling are exquisite, and he painted on and on obliviously, ignoring giants—ignoring Titian—and all he did, ignoring the revolutions going along around him, Carpaccio was simply a painter of gorgeous capuchin monkeys, while the world rockets to new heights.

RAPHELSON   (*Laughing.*)   Is that why you did it? Man. Really?

FABRICANT   Draw your own conclusions. I hated him. I hated his pretty little scenes of the fifteenth century equivalent to our shopping malls and holiday gift shop panoramas. I was passionate then about art which has aspirations and places the artist at risk, and I am more so now, so dismiss me, and make fun of me, and have as much contempt for me as you like, but understand, I am deadly serious about what I do, and you are squandering the enthusiastic support of someone who will do anything for what he believes in.

There is a moment.

RAPHELSON So you're a fuckin' crusader? Hey. I don't want to be a cause.

FABRICANT In which case, we are done, we are through, and there is nothing else to say except "Goodbye, Malcolm, I shall be taking Judd with me when I go this afternoon."

RAPHELSON How long were you in jail?

FABRICANT Six months in the loony bin and ten months in a prison in Essex. I am not allowed back to Spain for the rest of my life, and the Italians are fairly enthusiastic about my staying away too. It was worth it.

RAPHELSON The Carpaccio was destroyed?

FABRICANT No. Paint came right off within a few months. These people aren't total idiots.

RAPHELSON What—what was the lunatic asylum like?

FABRICANT First place I've ever been totally comfortable, frankly, and the sex is terrific. Do you know how sexual mad people are? All they want is to fuck in odd corners and under hedges. You haven't been? I recommend it. They feed you, the drugs are fun, and you should have *no* trouble getting in. Cheers.

He smiles at Raphe. He starts out.

RAPHELSON   Trevor. (*Gesturing towards the rack, and when he speaks again, it's a casual throwaway, a shrug, a sigh.*)   Fine, they're yours. You can take 'em.

FABRICANT   No, not good enough. We need the man himself, I'll need you in rooms with art people and their exhilarations. (*Beat.*)   You must come to New York as well.

END OF ACT ONE

ACT II

Four weeks have passed. A late afternoon rainstorm has cut through the torpor. Raphelson stands, looking, staring, at a clunky old orange rotary phone, which is RINGING insistently away. He is wearing a new linen suit the color of a field of winter wheat and a tie loosely around his neck. He looks perfectly ready for The Rialto. There is a suitcase on the landing. On the old turntable, Coltrane is playing softly. The portrait of Sara Raphelson remains exactly as it was, unfinished, untouched, since the prior scene. There is a rag draped over part of it, to further reinforce its total and utter abandonment by Raphelson—and Judd.

Also not inconspicuously placed is a large wooden crate, open, with one picture inside and room for more. Raphe finally picks up the phone.

RAPHELSON (*Into phone.*) Yeah, Trevor. I *know* you are standing at Idlewild, "in shock," you *told* me that ten *minutes* ago. (*Beat.*) I *know* it's called JFK now, but not by me. Son. (*Gently, but with a certain deadly aim.*) You really should go back to Manhattan, I'm obviously *not* on the plane, so there's no point in—waiting at the gate, is there? (*Beat.*) No. I will *not* leave here right "this moment." (*Beat.*) Well maybe it was a slight *mistake* calling it a "Retrospective." (*Beat. He cringes. He shrugs. He takes the earpiece away from his ear and looks at it.*) Everything you just screamed is very true. I am very happy about all this, it's wonderful, it's a *dream*. (*Beat. He nods.*) Nevertheless, screaming will not make me *magically* appear at baggage claim. (*Beat.*) No—do not come down here! (*He closes his eyes, desperate.*) No, no no. DO NOT. (*Beat.*) Judd. Yes. Well. I don't know where he is, he's probably gone to look

57

at some ruins, or perhaps to make some. Let's pick this up again tomorrow, go back to Manhattan now, Trevor. Yes, I am coming to New York—no, I won't do *anything to jeopardize all the*—yes. (*Bellowing.*)   I'm happy! Yes, I'm delirious, yes! Yes! Yes!

He hangs up and then, for good measure, kicks the receiver off the cradle. The record ends. He paces around the room.

RAPHELSON (*cont.*)   Motherfucker, Jesus. Fuck. I mean . . . really. Really. This fucking yenta from the Kalahari is . . . !

Julia has entered. Raphe stops. Casual.

RAPHELSON (*cont.*)   Wanna drink?

JULIA (*Entering, drenched.*)   Malcolm? What are you still doing here?

RAPHELSON   I left my toothbrush and some cunning little socks I like, so I turned around. I'm going tomorrow. (*Calmly.*)   I really hate this telephone.

JULIA   I can see that. I heard you yelling. I heard you from the intersection of San Sebastian and Cinco de Mayo actually. Did Judd stay too?

RAPHELSON   'Fraid so. He rather abruptly stormed off somewhere.

Julia looks to him—A gesture of "what happened?" He clinks her glass, shrugs.

RAPHELSON (*cont.*)   It's so hard for me to get drunk these days. It takes so much work.

They drink.

RAPHELSON (*cont.*)   Oh God. This day. Wow. Fabricant? He's in this dream state, he's in this elaborate, mirrored rococo revenge fantasy where the art world is going to come to a complete halt. Do a volte-face. Over me! (*Beat. He laughs.*)   It's so *fucking* touching and so *fucking* naive. But he's got me. He got me.

JULIA   Yes? Hooked you, has he?

RAPHELSON   He's turned it into a fucking dog and pony act—a goddamn *limo* showed up here right after you left this morning and it sat there in front, surrounded by laughing children throwing shit at it.

JULIA   You'd think he'd know better.

RAPHELSON   Yeah, you would, wouldn't you? Where did he find it? He must have called the drug lords and rented. And then *Judd,* who has been so much *fun* lately, just poof—vanishes—just can't . . . *take* it anymore, he's so . . . angry, so we're waiting—and—these crates and I cut my finger and—

JULIA   What's going on with him?

RAPHELSON   I dunno. Maybe it has something to do with New York. That fucking kid. Do you think in Quatroccento Italy, the assistants caused so much trouble? No, they mixed paints, stretched canvases, and answered phones. Maybe tomorrow I can actually get outta here.

JULIA   So you haven't changed your mind about going? (*Disappointed.*)   I thought maybe you had.

RAPHELSON (*Scoffing.*)   Please. I have a ticket and a room at the Lombardy Hotel. I have—a man from *The New York Times* called and we're supposed to have *lunch.* He saw slides of the old and the new stuff and is . . . (*Beat. He realizes that she is very drenched.*)   Look at you: You're soaked. Take those things off.

Raphelson gets a thin, worn blanket and hands it to her.

RAPHELSON (*cont.*)   You shouldn't go out on that lake when it's storming, the   lightning; every few years some kid gets fried up like a *relleno*.

Julia gestures for Raphe to turn around. He does so.

JULIA (*As she takes off her wet clothes and drapes the blanket over herself.*)   Yeah, well, I'm getting desperate. I tossed a coin into the water—an offering.

RAPHELSON (*Still not looking at her.*)   Desperation occasionally leads to grace.

JULIA   I like how the rain cools it down here, it's ten degrees cooler.

Beat.

RAPHELSON   May I turn around please?

JULIA   No . . . no . . . no . . . not yet. Okay, now. God, does this mean I have to say goodbye to you again?

He turns. There is a moment, both aware of her nakedness under the blanket.

RAPHELSON   Hi.

JULIA   Malcolm. You haven't touched this painting in four weeks. And. My moving in coincided with the end of your working.

RAPHELSON   The environmentalist has perhaps a theory . . . ?

JULIA   Don't be cunty. I upset the balance. Between you and Judd.

RAPHELSON   You? What? The *what*? (*Calmly.*)   You think I'm running an arts camp for upper-middle-class drug fiends on the run? You've probably never known a junkie before.

This is just boojie-junkie horseshit. I mean—four weeks . . . (*Angrily, gathering his evidence.*)   *Four weeks* of sulking, of brooding, of goddamn *wasted time!* On what? Accommodation! It's become clear to me that I can't work with him around. He's trying to push me out of my own . . . (*Suddenly, impetuously trying out a theory.*)   I don't think I'm gonna take him to New York.

JULIA   And yet he's still here. Why is that? Why did you not send him packing?

RAPHELSON (*An admission, grudging.*)   Because. He's got these certain skills. (*She raises an eyebrow as if to say "explain."*) But there's this battle going on in him. He's at a crossroads. He could either become a real actual person. Someone with his own goddamn testimony. Maybe even make his own work. Or he can go on in this long sad half-life, lost, and draining away the energy out of anyone who comes into his ambit, and only out of the desire for self-destruction, for revenge on life, health, creativity—

JULIA   Yes, well. I agree. But he's looking to you. Isn't he?

RAPHELSON   Yes but I chose *not* to have children, Julia.

JULIA   Probably a prudent choice. What're you so angry about?

RAPHELSON (*Frustrated.*)   *Why* the hell are we talking about *him?* I don't understand exactly why you're even concerned. He got you goin' too?

JULIA   I know all these kids who have been jettisoned by— you know—the *bored, you know,* fickle people who didn't know what to do with the children they had. Dropped foals. It's so American: At first, they're cute, like puppies. But after Christmas, everyone wants to drop 'em off at a shelter. So why are you being such a little bitch with Judd?

RAPHELSON   Excuse me? "Little bitch"? He's not here for an apprenticeship! He's not a fucking freshman in some fucking class—you think the world is like school. It's not! Not this world! It's all about erasure. I can't trust him with any of my secrets! He's got me so fucked up.

JULIA   But you don't trust anyone, Raphe, do you?

Quietly.

JULIA *(cont.)*   He's not your *hooker*, here to just "do" you. He's a boy. And you don't understand him. You make not the slightest attempt at—

RAPHELSON   Nevertheless, darling. It ain't my table. And I think the subject of Judd has been exhausted.

A tense silence ensues.

She nods. They smile. He pats her cheek. Getting up, he goes to the turntable, where the Coltrane has ended. Puts on another record.

RAPHELSON *(cont.)*   This is a *canción* from sometime around 1933. They're all about broken hearts, homesickness, and *langosta*. (*Beat.*)   . . . Wanna dance?

Julia getting up, still holding her drink, quiet, a throwaway.

RAPHELSON *(cont.)*   Always.

They dance slowly, both drinking, and he has a surprising courtliness, and old-fashioned grace. The rain pours down. It's still quiet and the rain is bigger than the people.

JULIA   I see you've never done this before, have you? You need a lesson. One foot never leaves the—

RAPHELSON *(A smile, interrupting.)*   Hey. You're a fine dancer. Relax.

Beat. As they dance slowly.

RAPHELSON (*cont.*)   When I was a kid, living in East L.A., there was a community center where they taught you Emma Goldman, table manners, and dancing. It was the *one* thing my wife truly appreciated about me: I was the only good commie with any rhythm.

JULIA   It's attractive; I can see why she'd overlook your less appealing qualities.

RAPHELSON   Not for very long. I was tolerated for just under a year, and of course, she met someone who made more sense. We used to exchange cards. Now I don't even know if she's still alive.

JULIA   And then you skipped down here. Where you waited for someone to rescue you.

RAPHELSON   Is this rescue? What's happening to me? That's funny. No. Before I came here, there was one last botched attempt at marriage. *She* hung around for *four* years, watching me pretend not to get bitter, watching our friends fall away, supporting us. Even when I had turned into an animal, she stayed two more years, which were two more than I had any right to expect.

JULIA   So . . . Had these women been less supportive, you're saying you might still be together? And the friends? Just too damn much empathy for you? Too many people watching you?

RAPHELSON (*Drinks, shrugs, dances.*)   Don't fall in love with an artist; it's all heartbreak, dereliction of duty, and pretending to listen. That's my advice. Don't fall in love at all, really.

JULIA   Hard. To. Do. I have a feeling you're not coming back here at all, are you?

RAPHELSON   You can have the keys. Stay as long as you like, I might be back with my tail between my legs and—

JULIA   (*She laughs, shaking her head.*)   Judd warned me this is where the demons live. No frogs. No art. All efforts thwarted. And you never even got around to *painting* me.

RAPHELSON   No.

Shakes his head.

RAPHELSON   (*cont.*)   Too hard, Julia. I don't want to lie to you. I'm stymied. You confuse issues, I don't know what I'm seeing when I look at you. I used to be able to work from photographs . . .

He gestures to the incomplete picture behind him.

RAPHELSON   (*cont.*)   But having someone sit for you causes all sorts of problems.

JULIA   (*Nodding.*)   But what you're not telling me is that you're scared of me.

RAPHELSON   (*Dry.*)   *Rivined* with terror. Okay. Sit down. Please. Take off that blanket. Please. Have a drink . . .

She lets the blanket fall. There is no comment from Raphe. She's suddenly naked. He goes to look for a pad of rough newsprint, some thick pencils. She sits. Raphe stares at her, as he tries to figure out the moment of starting.

JULIA   Malcolm. I didn't say anything this morning. They're going to order me back to Berkeley in about three minutes.

RAPHELSON (*Nodding. Not unexpected news.*)   And you'll go. Judd will go. I'll probably come back from New York in a while. Fix this place, the leaks, the caving roof.

JULIA   It'll be good. No more tiresome people to bug you, just *you*.

RAPHELSON (*Nodding.*)   The naps, the solitude, the roosters at dawn. The solitude. The naps . . .

JULIA (*Nodding.*)   ". . . The roosters at dawn." It sounds good to me.

RAPHELSON   I don't know. *Something's* happened. You learn to live in silence, and then suddenly this house is filled with this voluntary *life*. And you start thinking "Oh, I remember this, this is why people have friends, why they have lovers."

JULIA   Some people are bred for aloneness. I think I am.

Raphe rips the paper.

JULIA (*cont.*)   But . . . Could you live in New York? That's a place where you can be alone with millions of other people.

RAPHELSON   Gotta see if New York will have me.

JULIA   I don't see why not: It's still a Mecca for angry bearded men in strange outfits. You'll fit in nicely.

RAPHELSON   I'm less angry than I am curious.

JULIA   But you want to *leave*? Actually leave? Really? Is that why you've been so pissy?

RAPHELSON   I'm afraid rusticity may be starting to go stale on me.

JULIA   It gets pretty cold on Riverside Drive in February, chief.

RAPHELSON   You tryin' to tell me something, Jul?

JULIA (*Nodding.*)   Bring a warm coat. Don't slip on the ice. Watch out for loose women.

RAPHELSON   Julia. If you feel compelled to offer an opinion, do so: I can take it.

JULIA   Okay. I don't think you'll be very happy there, frankly, and I think you know that. And I don't understand.

RAPHELSON   So you think I should call it all off, huh?

A small smile. He shrugs, considering.

RAPHELSON (*cont.*)   You have no idea, Julia, how deeply satisfying it would be to take these paintings to New York and sell them to the people who did this to me.

JULIA   Revenge art, is it? Is that all this is?

Raphelson rips his second page and crumbles it.

RAPHELSON   Something wrong with that?

JULIA   I don't understand how you artists live with all this. These wars! Heights of ecstasy, depths of despair. It's so uneconomical. So exhausting. Fabricant, New York, Judd . . .

RAPHELSON   And you're a paragon of the cool and the rational? Sit still—how do you *not* go berserk with a man like Trevor Fabricant trying to build a casita in your asshole—I mean—you know.

Julia shrugs.

RAPHELSON (*Re the phone.*)   I can just hear him, that enraged sibilance—

JULIA   Yeah. A word of advice for when you go back to the States, homophobia is considered socially unattractive now, so you might want to—

RAPHELSON   (*Interrupting her.*)   You think I'm pissed off that those two kids is queer? Hell, everyone I *knew* was a fag. In my world? You never knew what you were getting, you'd go to an opening, end up going home with a goddamn rat terrier.

The phone suddenly RINGS, and without missing even a beat, Raphelson kicks the phone across the room, viciously. It's not funny.

RAPHELSON   (*cont.*)   (*Absolutely shockingly furious.*)   Christ! You expect me to work? With this? Do you, Julia?

He throws his pad of paper across the room. Yelling at the telephone.

RAPHELSON   (*cont.*)   I'm not drawing to make you people happy! I'm not a *sideshow*! *I can't work*! I can't work like this! I can't work. My hand can't do what my eye tells it to! I can't do it! You want to humiliate me? Is that it? Is this a *test*?

JULIA   What are you talking about?

RAPHELSON   (*A rush of words.*)   Fabricant says he can sell the lake painting for more money than I made from '63 to '92—*combined*.

JULIA   So what? I don't understand what's going on with you. You're telling me this would be some sort of compliment? Are you saying that would be an *affirmation*?

RAPHELSON   (*Avoiding the question.*)   It's as though I never did anything truly worthy until this kid arrived. Until Trevor promoted the thing. Now I'm . . . (*He looks at the box of paintings.*)   Maybe it would be better if none of these had ever been conceived.

JULIA   You don't want to go, do you?

RAPHELSON   Yes. No. Both. Both are valid. I don't know what to do.

JULIA   (*Shaking her head, disagreeing.*)   Stay tough, Malcolm.

RAPHELSON   I'm trying.

JULIA   (*Unblinking, but with a shrug, a throwaway.*)   Try harder. (*Suddenly very angry.*)   Try fucking harder, would you? Don't go all milky on me!

He looks at her, nonplussed.

JULIA   (*cont.*)   Don't sit here anesthetized! You rail and rage and bleed and fight every step of the day, you pretend to be crazier than rat shit, but it's all a cover.

RAPHELSON   (*Baffled.*)   I'm sorry. I didn't mean to upset you.

JULIA   (*Over him.*)   You have no idea what became of the country you left, it doesn't care about anything anywhere, even itself, even its children. Try fucking *harder*. Money? You came down here for thirty years and at the first sign of neon and room service and little men from the *Times,* you're suddenly about "more money than you made" between blah-blah and blah-blah? (*Beat.*)   Give it away if you're so disgusted. Give it to me! It's simple. I know where it'll do some good. But be honest. You want to go, and you want to win. Fine. (*Beat.*)   Don't go if you don't want to. Don't do anything you don't want to do, but for God's sake be honest with me.

RAPHELSON Honest with you: About?

JULIA In this moment. Needing each other.

RAPHELSON Fuckin' need. Huh? That's a tough one for me. Not my favorite word.

JULIA Which? Fucking or need?

There is a beat. He smiles. He considers. Nods.

RAPHELSON So what's your story? You seem to know how to handle everything, I mean, you're a fuckin' child, how'd you get to be so goddamn savvy?

JULIA (*Quietly, weary, fierce.*) You know what? You gotta stop doing that. You have *no* idea what I am. And I am many things, but a child isn't one of them.

She says nothing for a moment. He stares at her. He nods.

RAPHELSON Not a child—but—The problem is—

JULIA But—You turn me into one, don't you? I was married when I was eighteen. It's like waking up with a tattoo. You think "How did *this* happen." And you know who he was? He was basically Judd. He had illustrated an article I was writing on "concentric circles of responsibility"—little pencil scratchings—he got it, all the ramifications—and it ate him alive—he saw it so clearly—in the atavistic muck and the sand, and all the inhabitants of a one-foot tidal pool at Point Reyes, he saw what we had become. He was not from this planet *at all*. Fury, shooting up, binges, first as a joke, and then seriously. Anyway. I'm not a child.

RAPHELSON (*He sits down.*) So we both have failed marriages.

She shakes her head, gets up, covers herself with the blanket and pours herself another drink. There's a long moment. The rain comes down harder and harder.

JULIA (*Flat.*)   He threw himself off the roof of a hotel in The Tenderloin.

Beat. Raphe does not know what to do.

JULIA (*cont.*)   We were nineteen. Cut his wrists first. That hadn't worked, so then he jumped while I was out looking for him all night.

RAPHELSON   Jesus.

JULIA (*Shaking her head, bitter.*)   In and out of facilities. One week clean, then not. Tried to save himself through work on a children's book, but he never could get it down, and I tried and tried and got angrier and more tired, and he got more and more guilty and humiliated. Then one night he's dead outside a Pakistani restaurant we liked for the goat, and I'm pregnant. I go to my parents for help. No idea what to do. My dad, they'd been at Berekely, they'd both been in SDS, now they're both corporate lawyers—suggested "Well, have an abortion: we're pro-choice," my mom suggests "put it up for adoption." *No one—no one—* suggested I perhaps keep this baby or really even offered to help.

RAPHELSON   And . . . what did you do?

JULIA   I opted for the abortion. I regret it every day, because I want a kid. I went in. And I thought I would feel something. Anything—feel regret or freedom or release or *rage.* But I went to the clinic in Oakland, and came home, and I felt nothing. I felt numb. One of the walking dead of my time. Watched TV for two years straight. Seventies sitcoms. I finally fit in perfectly. *Finally* I was like everyone else. Nothing much mattered. '82, '83, '87 . . . I had gone dead like the place I lived in.

She smiles at him.

JULIA (*cont.*)   You want to know why I was so . . . *happy* to come here and live with you? Because you were born before this *ice age* hit, and you never gave up. My husband did. But under the wreckage and the disaffection and the rage, he was a gentle soul. I know that voice, and I love it.

Beat. Trying—successfully—not to cry; even stronger.

JULIA (*cont.*)   I like you so much, Raphe; please don't do anything you don't want to do.

RAPHELSON   What do you suggest?

JULIA   Be honest. There's something you refuse to tell me, there's some bluster about something, and I don't know what it is. Make a *choice*. You pay either way.

RAPHELSON (*Gently.*)   In that case, I choose this.

He goes to her and gently kisses her. She responds. There is a long moment.

JULIA (*She smiles.*)   Judd told me a month ago this was going to happen. I was waiting.

RAPHELSON   Were you? Sorry. (*A shrug.*)   I'm not very good with deadlines. (*He kisses her again.*)   Probably—The smart thing in my case, Julia, would be to take another stab at art, rather than at life. That part of my life may be over. I think. I hope. Given that one of my organs is likely to fail any day now.

JULIA That doesn't sound like very much fun.

They kiss again.

JUDD (*In the doorway, very, very wasted.*) Hey, I'd pay to see either one, art or life failing. (*He smiles at Julia.*) Hey, sweetie. So I was right, he finally close the deal with you?

JULIA (*Taking in his condition, wary.*) Hi, Judd. How's it going? Are you okay?

JUDD I'm happy, we get to leave, as soon as we work out all the false starts and shit, there's gonna be a trip to Moscow, know what I mean?

RAPHELSON (*A weary sigh.*) Here we go. You have a good day?

JUDD Oh yeah. Took a bus ride. The beach, Puerto Escondido. Lay on the sand, met some kids from Orange County, they even invited me on an expedition to find "the best beach on the Pacific, dude."

RAPHELSON It's a good offer. Maybe you oughta take them up on it.

JUDD Nah. It'd be a step down from the important work we're engaged in here. (*Takes in the crate.*) Gettin' these guys up to the big city. And we do have an efficient line of production to keep up, don't we? That's what we should call it. Many artists do it, I should be less . . . rigid. I'm so *fuckin'* rigid, man . . .

RAPHELSON (*Making a decision.*) Let's get you to bed.

He moves towards Judd, tries to guide him gently towards his room.

JUDD (*Pulling violently away.*) Fuck off.

Raphelson stands back. Judd smiles. He turns to Julia.

JUDD (*cont.*) Julia, he's evil. He's actually evil. What he's done.

JULIA How so?

JUDD (*Over her.*) You don't see it but he's conned you too, Julia. (*Miserable.*) I knew he would, I know what you think of me, but . . .

RAPHELSON Do you really want to do this in front of her? (*He looks to Julia.*) Judd seems to be suffering from an hallucination of provenance, Julia. It started off as a joke between us.

JUDD That part is true.

RAPHELSON Which I may have started. And now it's a full-blown psychosis.

JUDD What a small-time, penny-ante pig you are.

The next beat is an ascending rapid fire of overlaps.

RAPHELSON I don't know what it is you want!

JUDD Take a guess, there's a couple options!

RAPHELSON I have no idea what it is you think you're owed!

JULIA (*Starting out the door.*) I don't think you need me here, for this. I'll go.

JUDD Please, Julia, please stay.

She stops. Beat.

JUDD (*Turns back to Raphelson.*) It's a matter of respect, isn't it?

RAPHELSON (*To Julia.*) You see, Julia. The question he's posed, the question which has so successfully halted the work I came back to after so long—is "How to calculate the billable hours for saving this old man?"

To Judd.

RAPHELSON (*cont.*)   And you're always tabulating. Every time you enter this room, there's impatience and your barely suppressed appetite for domination. Which is, let me assure you, Judd, not a fight you can win.

JUDD   No. No. Not domination, not even gratitude, I don't need any of *that*. Just not *erasure*, *dismissal*, and *contempt*.

RAPHELSON   Why did you even come here? (*Laughing, exhausted by this.*)   Think about it. What you're holding over me: the interrogations and corrections, the satisfaction you derive from what I'm doing—not on *my* behalf, but rather, the implication, which grows less and less subtle, that *I* am *your* assistant. Julia, do you see—?

Julia sits down in the armchair, not wanting to referee.

JUDD   I'm just talking about acknowledgment, is all. (*He laughs.*)   None, not a moment of it. Not here.

Beat. Raphelson can't answer. Judd sees, presses the point home very simply.

JUDD (*cont.*)   Acknowledgment that you could afford to be generous. Acknowledgment that you might owe me the courtesy of instruction, and that I was worth your trust, but there has been none of that.

RAPHELSON   Really?

JUDD   Yes. You talk about contempt: You were the one who placed me neatly in the roll of lost cause and local schmuck. I came down here willing to listen and you turned me into your little smart-ass bitch. (*Very upset.*)   I actually hate you for that. I'm probably twenty times smarter than you think but it's easier for you to treat me like a threat.

Raphelson is silent. Judd shakes his head. Goes on quietly.

JUDD (*cont.*)   How could you expect me not to resent you: You give nothing. Not a moment of recognition that there's another person deeply involved here, and that this person actually did something while you slept, pissed, moaned, and drank! And while you did those things *so* well, *I worked and worked!*

RAPHELSON (*Looking up at the painting of his mother.*)   You forget all the details. You don't know what it means to know two million things at the same time. All the details. The hands. Little things: buttons, smudges, *dynamism*!

JUDD   That's what you're holding on to? Your ability to render ornamentation and filigree? That's what you consider to be your work? These meaningless details?

RAPHELSON   This woman. Do you know anything about her? The times I still talk to her in this room. How much I miss her. I'm three quarters of a century old and I still miss her! What did she smell like. Tell me. Lemons or lavender or sweat and tobacco and castile soap? (*He presses home the point.*)   Which one of us is the parasite? It's what the drugs and ruination are all about: You want to have squandered something in order to reclaim it, but you have nothing to say. You're my illustrator. You're no painter.

Or else you'd be making your own work. Christ, if you're so brilliant, why do you need me? Where's *your* work?

JUDD   Right there!

He makes a sweeping gesture, taking in the entire room.

JULIA (*Emphatic.*)   This is unbearable, both of you, the desolation, the bloodshed—don't.

RAPHELSON (*After a moment.*)   Judd. Figure out if you have anything to paint about. Figure out who you are, because right now, all you are is a magpie, a mynah bird. You're me, minus the self.

JUDD   You're far too easy on yourself; *you're you* minus the self. (*He picks up a crumbled piece of paper.*)   Julia, I don't care if you believe me or not, but take a look. This is what he can do.

He shows her one of Raphe's abandoned attempts at drawing, just some tense markings.

JUDD (*cont.*)   Unintelligible broken lines. It's dead. (*To Raphe.*)   And you hate yourself for it, and can't afford to share how much you know, because you think I'm a thief. Pathetic. Plenty of people keep working after the style of the moment changes. Do you want me to name some?

RAPHELSON (*Casual, but deeply angry, he's faking it.*)   Nah, I know all that. I can tell you who did what. We should've had this out a long time ago, pal. I'm going to finish this picture on my own and go up to New York *on my own, with them,* without you by my side, with that shitty little grin on your face. I'm going to go up there, and let Trevor do what he's promised.

Picks up the envelope of cash left by Fabricant, from out of a drawer.

RAPHELSON (*cont.*)   Take it, get back to New York on your own, or go wherever, Chiapas is nice, you're fired.

Judd does nothing. Raphelson suddenly flings the envelope at him, and after hitting Judd in the chest, he picks it up and flings it right back; money flies everywhere.

JULIA (*Distraught.*)   All right, that's enough—

JUDD (*In tears, over her.*)   I don't need a handout, pal, goddamn you, you can tell yourself anything you want but you and I know what really happened here, that fucking drawing Fabricant sold for all this money—are you gonna tell this woman you did *that*? (*Beat.*)   There's no way I could forgive you for what you've done to me.

Holds out his hands, maybe a foot apart, like showing the size of a caught fish.

JUDD (*cont.*)   I just wanted *this* much from you.

He exits. There is silence.

JULIA   They're his? He painted them?

RAPHELSON   I worked for Diego Rivera once. I was a kid. There were six apprentices, six assistants. There's a fresco a few hundred miles from here. It has Rivera's name on it, but it was painted by me. The man took credit for all his assistant's considerable work; he was a monster. My God, the guy painted with a gun in his belt. It was hilarious. The endless self-promotion and bombast. But I tried to figure out what his mode was. What his testimony was.
    I listened and watched and was in awe of him. That's the way it's done. I did not try and destroy him in the process.

JULIA   They're not his, these paintings are not his, right?

RAPHELSON   How could they be? My concerns, my people, my memory, and my history.

JULIA   But he painted them.

She thinks for a moment.

JULIA (*cont.*)   I had a professor, he folded all of his students' work into his own researches, which was fine, but he did it in the most scurrilous underhanded way, because he wanted a big book and revenge, and when he got that stuff, it didn't make him feel all that much better. I watched that one too. That was cancer, believe me. He folded up and what had been just bitterness became bone-deep cynicism and then all that was good was finally bad. He got recognition, money, a box at the opera, whatever. This will kill you, Raphe. You're better than that. It's why Judd wants to be like you.

RAPHELSON   Poor guy. I'm sure he was in hell. I'd pity him, but since I know what *that* feels like, I won't bother. Let me tell you something. Listen to me.

Finally, quietly.

RAPHELSON (*cont.*)   It's impossible, you know. To come back to painting when you've been gone from it for any length of time.

Beat.

RAPHELSON (*cont.*)   It's just never done.

Beat.

RAPHELSON (*cont.*)   Everything goes.

JULIA   Yes, *more* than everything, *absolutely* everything. You'll be left with nothing at all.

RAPHELSON   Thanks for the cautionary tale, I think I need to work it out by myself. There have been far too many people in here, that's obviously been the problem.

JULIA   True. (*She starts to gather her belongings and get out.*) I'll be out of here in as long as it takes to pack.

RAPHELSON   What do you want, Julia?

JULIA (*Gently.*)   You are . . . an obviously lovely man, Malcolm. But you've no skill at being kind and being generous. The signal to noise ratio is just way way off.

She exits. Raphelson is alone in the studio. There is silence.

LIGHTS FADE

SCENE TWO

The studio, two days later, just before dawn, the light is ink going to ochre; it's the light of a kind of hell. Judd, in an astonishing state of dishevelment, enters the studio and collapses on to the sofa. He is shaking, and bruised. Fabricant follows him, appalled. He is carrying a cup of coffee and is once again dressed in an expensive, though by now somewhat soiled, English summer suit.

FABRICANT   No, no—no.

He moves Judd up from the sofa and puts him in the chair.

FABRICANT (*cont.*)   There'll be no coddling you, Judd. Drink your . . . beverage, we have to start moving.

JUDD   I'm going to need several more cups. Even to think about moving. That cell. God. It was amazing. As far as jail cells go, it was somewhere in the Max Ernst–Hieronymus Bosch latitudes.

FABRICANT   I am insisting that this be done with a bit of grace.

JUDD   Hey, I'm all for grace. A dying fall. A silent, dignified exit.

Judd dips a piece of bread into his coffee. Fabricant watches him, truly appalled.

79

FABRICANT   Well, it's too late for that. Raphelson's holed himself up in his room, you're back on heroin—where's the dignity? It's a fucking calamity. Look. The police were very kind to let you go, but we do have a ticking clock. You have to be out of town by tonight. For God's sake, you were lying in the town square shooting up in front of the *turistas,* Judd!

JUDD   (*Outraged.*)   I shot up in the movie theater, not the square!

Trevor just stares at him. Beat. Calmer.

JUDD   (*cont.*)   How much did you have to bribe them to get me out?

FABRICANT   (*Picking up the money which is strewn about the studio floor.*)   Not a little but less than I thought. Because when all is said and done, they're businessmen too, aren't they? Yes. . . . They came at me with palm outstretched, let me tell you, and not just the police, but the fire chief as well, and then a lady from the Governor's Office of Film Production. Whatever that is.

JUDD   (*Eying Trevor's suit.*)   Well it doesn't help when you show up looking like Buster Keaton's wispy little sister.

FABRICANT   Just finish your wet, soaked coffee-bread and let's get these things crated up. They should have all gone up North weeks ago. (*He puts down the fistful of cash.*)   I let this thing go on and on and on . . . The silence and the elliptical nonsense.

Fabricant takes a small painting out of the rack—a self-portrait of Malcolm, all defiance and rage and blackness.

JUDD   Wait a second. I told you he didn't paint these.

FABRICANT Who is ever going to believe that? You've never painted anything remotely like this.

He holds up the painting.

JUDD (*Astonished.*) Hold on, back the fuck up, pal. I can prove it.

FABRICANT This is him. This is Malcolm Raphelson. How would you presume to know this much about him? How?

JUDD I can do them in my sleep. I can paint this down to the brush stroke . . . !

FABRICANT That doesn't mean a thing. It doesn't prove anything. We know you're skilled. It means nothing. You don't seem to have a handle on the thorny nature of the problem. These are sold, you see. I've *sold* them, I've taken money already and I don't have it to give back.

JUDD No you're kidding me, you're not—

FABRICANT (*Over Judd.*) I *promoted* this man. There's a woman coming to the gallery, there's a woman from *Vogue* . . . And a hobgoblin from *Art News*! Not to mention a eunuch from the BBC with a tape recorder and bad breath!

JUDD Are you *seriously* saying that you could . . . ?

FABRICANT I mean, come on. Isn't it just a little bit too much for me to buy? The notion that you did everything? I mean, come on. Think about it.

JUDD How can you hand these over to people? Sell them. Knowing that they're fakes?

FABRICANT Are they? They don't look fake to me. And after all, there is the larger question of what is fraud, exactly . . . ?

JUDD (*Laughing, thrilled.*)   "What is fraud?" Is that what you just asked . . . ?

FABRICANT   So he had some help. Whatever help you offered was voluntary, wasn't it?

JUDD   My God. You actually have no level you refuse to sink below, do you?

FABRICANT   You volunteered, and now you have some proprietary issues, well, too bad! That hardly makes them any less authentic than anything else in the world. They're wonderfully done, the colors are marvelous. They're glorious surfaces . . .

JUDD   Thank you.

FABRICANT   (*Ignoring this.*)   He's being described as "an American original."

JUDD   (*A small shrug and a laugh of disgust.*)   He could have been. But he ain't. Someone may be, but I dunno . . .

FABRICANT   Look. You have a shot. I have another one of these baby-sitting jobs lined up, and he's very docile, and he's in bloody Woodstock, I'll hand it to you, for God's sake—

JUDD   (*Laughing.*)   You have another old fuckin' fraud, dude? Is that gonna be your new schtick? Hey, niche marketing, all for it . . .

FABRICANT   Don't make this into your ticket to bitterness and larceny. Really. For God's sake, start your life. It's getting very, very late.

JUDD   I was trying. Then you sent me down here.

FABRICANT   If this is . . . If this is a Judd Sturgess scheme for money . . . if that's what this is, I'm telling you right now, I haven't got any.

JUDD (*Delighted, as though it had just dawned on him.*)   It's a *moneymaking scheme*. I have you exactly where I want you. How much? How much do I get? Seventy-five percent . . . ?

FABRICANT   Do you know how people pay for art? In bits and pieces. The richer they are, the smaller the bits. I mean, I've got people buying stuff on account probably until I'm in a fucking casket. Tiny little checks. So you can't hold me up. As it is, I'm going to have to go back to Cape Town and beg for a loan. A very new and marvelous low for me.

JUDD   I don't care about money.

FABRICANT   You don't care about money? That is one of the more outré lies you've ever—my God, I mean, have you forgotten the nice man at Barneys snipping your credit card into a hundred pieces—look . . . We can work out a little bonus once we're out of here but I won't negotiate down here. I hate it here.

JUDD   You are not hearing this, are you? We are so NOT in a negotiation.

FABRICANT   I'm offering you a chance to clean up. You've only got me. Because if I drop you, it's either death, a long sojourn in a Mexican jail, or if you're very, very lucky, a ditch in San Diego. Hustling for dirty needles outside a Burger King. If you continue to make claims.

JUDD   Yikers.

FABRICANT   Judd, I'm sorry but there's no way for you to come out the winner here. Do you follow? There's no way. What you say can never be proven. Do you understand?

JUDD   I think so. You're saying that you believe me . . .

FABRICANT   (*Over this.*)   Nope, sorry.

JUDD   (*Over him.*)   But while still vaguely interested in notions of right and wrong, in the abstract, they're moot here, because you have to back your horse, the great betrayer.

FABRICANT   (*Picking up the small painting.*)   Did you—I have only one question. There is only one question: Did you forge his signature?

JUDD   Did I forge his signature? Jesus. Trevor. Who are you?

FABRICANT   Right. Didn't think so. He signed. This is Malcolm's signature, is it not?

Beat. Judd does not answer. There is a moment. Fabricant has won. Judd stands there, defeated.

FABRICANT   (*cont.*)   You know what? I'm tired of it. You've become one of those people one regrets. (*Fervent and raw.*)   You kissed me, Judd. After all the pathetic contortions I went through to fall out of love with you, the exercises in *self-control* I had to practice—to clear you out of my head—sending you to fucking bloody hideous foul Mexico—so you'd be gone from the Lower East Side—after humiliating myself again and again, you actually *kissed* me! (*Beat. He is distraught.*) And I of course—took that, stupidly—as a favorable sign. Idiotic. Simply pathetic of me. To think that you might actually be . . . (*Beat. He shakes his head, weary.*)   You're so dangerous. You seduce people to get ahead.

JUDD   (*Done.*)   To get . . . ahead? Hey, well, it really worked, didn't it? I mean, *look* at me. Okay?

Judd sits. Raphelson enters. Judd sees him and moans.

FABRICANT (*Seeing Raphelson entering.*)   Malcolm. Thank God. This is a ghastly mess . . .

RAPHELSON   Is that how you'd describe it? (*Shaking his head at the state of Judd.*)   Jesus. God. Look at you. Man. The cops hit you? Looks like they banged you up pretty good. You must have been disrespectful to the wrong Federale.

Raphelson goes to the table, to get his bottle of mescal.

FABRICANT   I suppose I owe you an apology, don't I? I promise you, it's not even a question in my mind. I know exactly who's responsible for these, please forgive him— Judd's not well. You keep thinking that people can be rehabilitated and they can. But it takes time. And I should not have involved you.

RAPHELSON   No. You should not have.

JUDD   May I say something?

FABRICANT (*Fierce.*)   No, you bloody well may not ever say anything again! Not a word! You've done quite enough. We have to pack all this up . . . (*He indicates the racks of paintings.*)   . . . and catch a plane.

RAPHELSON   This has turned into a salvage operation for you, hasn't it, Trevor?

FABRICANT   Not at all. Complications arise. The end is in sight. These problems are sorting themselves out, we need only move through the moment . . .

RAPHELSON   A little Zen Buddhism from Cape Town? Trevor. I wonder if I could ask you to do a favor for me.

FABRICANT   Of course.

RAPHELSON   Go down the street, please. The little market. Señora Farol's.

FABRICANT   (*Not sure of what is being asked of him.*)   You— you—want me to go to the market for you?

RAPHELSON   Yeah. If we're gonna pack this stuff—I need razors, and a bottle of mescal, and see if she has my mail while you're there, okay? Also some Manzanilla tea. It'll be good for him.

FABRICANT   (*Flustered.*)   Tea, mescal, razors—and—and—and *mail?* Anything else?

RAPHELSON   Perhaps you might be so good as to pay her a little something on my account . . . ? Say two grand.

Fabricant is trying to process all the signals—he looks over at Judd, who is sitting in the chair, and indicates he should follow him.

FABRICANT   Judd—?

RAPHELSON   No, he stays. We'll be fine. I'll stay with him. I'll watch him.

Fabricant exits. Raphelson and Judd are alone.

RAPHELSON   (*cont.*)   This tea they have is good for the shakes.

JUDD   I don't need anything from you.

RAPHELSON   Julia's gone back to the lake.

JUDD   (*Quietly, finally.*)   You thought . . . you could keep her. And she got sick of you too, right? Cleared out. Well—she saw through you and couldn't face you anymore. She has character. You were right, she has character, she's "the great American girl," smart, funny, and doesn't have to be nice.

Beat.

JUDD (*cont.*)   Did you ever consider a career in public office when you were younger? You could've done all this pointless demolition on a much more gratifying scale.

RAPHELSON (*Staring at Judd, deadly serious. He sits down close to him.*)   Judd. Is the point of what you're doing to die?

JUDD (*Refusing or unable to look at Raphe.*)   I'd say it's on the table, but no, not as soon as you might like.

RAPHELSON   You sure?

JUDD   Not right now. Sorry. (*Beat.*)   I don't want to be dead, I just want . . .

RAPHELSON   I'm trying to say that I'd hate to see you succeed at that.

JUDD   Shut up. I just want one thing: To know *why?* (*Beat.*) *Why* on earth did you do this to me? Look at me. This is what you've done.

Beat. Raphelson cannot speak.

JUDD (*cont.*) (*Totally articulate and clearheaded. He goes on, shaking his head, still baffled.*)   *Why?* Malcolm. The public nature of it. As soon as there were other people to witness this—you turned—The satisfaction. You made fun of me with Trevor, to my face, and worse, with her too.

   Any opportunity for indignity, humiliation: "Cabbages for hands," erasure, rewriting history to your own specs . . . why? All the things you hated. The prospect of New York. Of what you would do to me—at a retrospective, in a *gallery*. Yow. I can imagine it—your constant digs and with so many people there—I don't understand it. I don't. Can you please try and explain it.

Beat. Judd is in tears. He shakes his head.

JUDD (*cont.*)   I'm sorry if I . . . (*Beat.*)   *Did* something—if I seemed—*disrespectful* or . . . (*Beat. There is silence. Judd tries to pull himself together. Raphelson is watching him very closely. He shakes his head.*)   I keep trying to figure out why you would *possibly* want to do this and I can't even— (*Beat.*) I wasn't around for all the years you watched yourself become invisible and more and more marginal . . . It must have been . . . (*He stops. He nods. Suddenly clear to him.*) I know what it is. (*Beat. Simply amazed.*)   Take *my* work— sell it . . . and sell it as your own—and you get your revenge on everyone—me—because I can actually paint—and these people whom you loathe, who did this to you. It's so malignant. It's brilliant and twisted. You get everything you want. That's what this is. Revenge on all of us.

Pause. Raphe says nothing.

JUDD (*cont.*)   You're a comic book villain, do you know that, Malcolm? And in case you hadn't noticed—up there—back in New York, they've declared that painting is dead. You have no idea how tiny the stakes are. (*Judd is suddenly absolutely certain and direct and compelled*.)   But you know who I am? I am a mute with great feeling, huge battles going on inside, storms, plagues . . . but no way to express any of it. These useless *skills*. To execute a . . . but otherwise impotent, nothing else.

Beat.

JUDD (*cont.*)   I loved you Malcolm, I would sit here and understand exactly what you wanted, what you were trying to do. Just a nod or a shake or twitch from you was enough. Fantastic. Magic. Collaboration, the sum bigger than the two parts, I was never better, you were never braver—and however it worked—when we were together, something great—But then, alone, when I went off, I went through pad after pad, now I was fucked . . . but all of it a blur, worthless. Dead. Nothing to say. Torn paper.

RAPHELSON (*Looking at the paintings.*)   Well, then, wouldn't you say we're in the same boat then, wouldn't you say?

JUDD   Then why? Please. Why was I the..?

RAPHELSON (*Directly. Quietly.*)   Because you were there. (*Beat.*)   You have such gifts. If you could just . . . comprehend . . . (*He stops. He can't find the words.*) . . . Can you move?

JUDD (*Bone tired, shaking his head.*)   What you got planned for me, now, Mal . . . don't. You win, it's fine, it's over.

RAPHELSON   Yeah. (*Beat.*)   Let's get to work, kid.

Raphelson goes to the rack and picks up the Lake painting, and starts out of the studio with it. Judd watches him.

LIGHTS FADE

SCENE THREE

Dusk. All the paintings are gone. Raphelson enters. He is carrying a large pot of chicken and rice, sets it on the table. The studio looks and feels emptied out. He goes to the turntable, puts on a record; He sits down and begins slowly sharpening thick pointless pencils methodically, with a knife.

Julia enters. She takes in the empty rack where the paintings were.

JULIA (*Finally, quietly.*)   Hi.

RAPHELSON (*Looks up. He smiles.*)   Huh. Well. You're back.

JULIA (*Tense.*)   I'm not staying—I just left some stuff here.

She indicates her clothes, left on the sofa from two nights ago, and begins to gather them.

RAPHELSON (*Gently.*)   Ah. Of course. Can we discuss your leaving here. Please?

JULIA   Well, yeah—I took you at your word. You said you wanted some time to work this out alone. (*She takes in the empty rack of paintings.*)   . . . And apparently you have, haven't you?

RAPHELSON (*As she looks at the empty rack.*)   Yes. I think I have.

JULIA   Clearly. (*She shakes her, done with it.*)   Look, Raphe. I'm done. They're sending someone else to wrap things up.

RAPHELSON   Oh—What about the frogs?

JULIA   The frogs. Well. Hey. Who knows? I found one finally. Torn up, long dead, mostly digested, in the guts of one of those bass. I keep killing fish, it's mostly assassination on my part and as such, satisfying, but who knows—there's some of them, out there, waiting somewhere—hiding.

RAPHELSON   Waiting for safe passage.

JULIA   Whatever. You don't really give a flying fuck about frogs, Raphe, do you? Or anything else really, for that matter, do you?

RAPHELSON   Julia—

JULIA (*Over him.*)   You should definitely go back to the States, they're ready for you now, you'll do so well; the weak and selfish men will make way for you, and you can be their hero, because in fact, you're brilliant at it. Go up,

90

be a roving fraud, working a con, perfectly planned by your little South African Barnum. (*Beat. Contempt.*)   Go back. You *are* America.

Another dead white male power monger, makin' his way on the backs of the people he's ruined, but doing it all in the name of something you call "art"? I was under the misapprehension that art was supposed to be . . . (*Astonished.*)   What were you thinking? (*She indicates the empty racks.*)   Because they may not have been his, but they weren't yours either.

RAPHELSON (*Nodding.*)   Yes. That is exactly right. Yes.

Judd enters, stumbling in, in his underwear, still very beat up.

RAPHELSON (*cont.*)   Judd. Look who's here.

JUDD   Hi. Hey, Julia, how are you . . . ?

He covers himself with a blanket.

JULIA (*Astonished to see him.*)   Judd, honey are you . . . ?

RAPHELSON   You didn't drink your tea, kid. You've got to finish it.

JUDD (*Shaking his head "no," he sits down.*)   I can't. The stuff tastes of rehab.

RAPHELSON   Julia. We're going to eat. I've made a little dinner. You're more than welcome to stay.   •

Raphelson, in a slow and ritualistic way, puts three plates out on the work table, glasses, etc., flanking the pot.

JULIA (*Astonished.*)   You're going to . . . what?

JUDD   I can't eat, really, no . . .

RAPHELSON   You've got to get something inside you. It's the only way. (*To Julia, who is watching in amazement.*)   This may be our last supper. Judd's gonna have to go tomorrow unless I can be persuasive with some very tough-looking policewomen.

JULIA I'm sorry but—I don't understand . . .

RAPHELSON They're—oh it's just a total matriarchy down here. These female cops look like Zapotec stone statues: They scare the men to death. It's a good system. The guys are kept in line pretty much.

JUDD They told me I have to leave, Mal! They'll throw me back in their pit!

RAPHELSON Yeah, well, we'll see about that. They like me. I'm family. I know them all.

JULIA (*Furious.*) The paintings! The paintings! My God—what have you done with them? You let him send them up?

JUDD (*Baffled.*) . . . Did I let him send them? (*Turning to Raphelson.*) You—you didn't tell her?

RAPHELSON (*To Julia.*) I owe you a rowboat. The paintings are at the very bottom of Lake Grijalva.

JULIA What?

RAPHELSON We sent them to the bottom, we cut them up, put them in the dinghy, set the whole thing on fire, and we watched. (*Beat.*) And that's that story. Finis.

JULIA You burned them? In my dinghy?

JUDD (*Numb. Nodding.*) I helped him. It was really very Goth. The burning boat, the steaming water, the wood cracking, all that canvas in flames.

RAPHELSON You might want to look to your tendency to leap to the wrong conclusions, Julia.

JULIA   You set my rowboat alight? The paintings and my boat?

JUDD   A sacrifice.

RAPHELSON   Probably an empty one: People have been offering things into that lake for centuries. But nothing happens.

JULIA   (*She looks around the room. There is a moment. Silence. Then a statement.*)   You didn't keep any of them.

RAPHELSON   Not even a scrap.

Julia sits down beside Judd.

JUDD   (*Shaking his head.*)   Poor Trevor. He just walked away. Came in, they were gone, we'd done it. It was just like a traffic pile-up in his head. I think it finished him off. I'll have to . . .

RAPHELSON   (*Sitting down next to Judd.*)   Oh, he'll be fine. He'll move on. Things happen so fast in the States.

JULIA   All that work, the vitriol. The battles. (*Beat.*)   I didn't quite see it ending like that.

RAPHELSON   We tried to work out some sort of custody arrangement, but in the end, what else was there to do?

JUDD   I . . . wanted to keep one. But we couldn't decide which. So they all went. (*He tries to smile, but he can barely speak.*)   There's absolutely nothing to show for all this. Nothing's left.

Julia hugs Judd, holding him. Raphelson takes in Judd's helpless despair, Julia trying to comfort him.

JULIA   Judd.

JUDD   (*Trying to laugh.*)   I'm sorry. (*Pulling himself together. He*

93

smiles.)   I don't know what to do. I actually have no idea. What do I do now? Any advice?

RAPHELSON   I once was an artist, in a particular time, which was about a particular struggle which I found compelling. The redistribution of wealth, Karl Marx, and sugarplum fairies. (*Beat.*)   If history is memory, then history edits out lives with ruthless abandon; first as farce, and then as tragedy. You have not been a *maker* of history; instead, history has unmade *you*. You are now the unseen hand, working on a mammoth-sized canvas, never to be heard of, or from, never to be seen. (*He looks at Judd, and there is a moment.*)   Then you're in a desert, and there's just two ways out: You can either make a leap, fuck fear, and God and man, or if you're weak and outta gas, you do horrible things. You become a brute. You once painted them, but now you are them: the foreman of some dark satanic mill, whom you put in the corner of the picture, whom you presented as something less than human. And you remember the day you painted that man, and wondered "How'd he get that way." (*He pours wine into the cheap juice glasses, and holds one up.*)   And if you're lucky, and able to receive the help of others, you might find out. (*Beat.*) Let's eat. Let's have dinner.

They come to the dinner table. There is a moment of gathering. Raphelson and the others are arranging the table.

RAPHELSON (*cont.*)   Last night, after we did it—I couldn't breathe. I couldn't sleep, I couldn't drink—I had to walk around. I ended up at the square around midnight. I just sat there. Know those crazy dogs that run around by the *mercado*? The ones that look like they're waiting for candy, or sex or something? They're always smiling, like they're scheming some bank heist or orgy or something . . .

And this one dog comes by and he looks at me like he was just waiting. He's waitin' for me to do something . . .

94

he doesn't want candy or pussy or a bone. He's just waiting. For me. To tell him the secret. (*Beat.*) So I tried to draw him. I drew him.

JUDD You drew a dog?

RAPHELSON Just a little drawing.

JUDD (*Showing some interest.*) Well then, come on, man. Let me see it. (*Beat.*) You don't want to hide your light under a bushel.

Raphelson looks in the pocket of his coat, takes out a torn, grease-smeared brown paper bag, which has been folded up. He hands it to Judd.

JUDD (*Looking at it. There is a long moment. Judd reluctantly shakes his head.*) . . . This is *terrible*. This is a terrible drawing.

They all laugh. It's so easy and convivial.

RAPHELSON (*Smiling.*) Yes. It is. Isn't it? It's done with the hand of a five year old. (*Beat. Gently.*) . . . You can have it. It's a gift. Maybe I'll go back . . . see if that mutt's still waiting . . . (*He looks around at the empty room. Beat. Quietly. Beat. He thinks.*) It's fleeting, you know. For most of us, it's very fleeting.

Once upon a time, I made some pictures. I had a name for myself, a title, all that. It evaporates and then you're left with this: (*He smiles.*) Three people. A drink, and a meal. (*He stands over the pot, shaking his head. Quietly, apologetic.*) And even though it's not enough, it will have to do. (*He raises his glass.*) To last suppers.

Lights fade on the three of them around the table.

END OF PLAY